Over Forty

Feeling Great and Looking Good!

by **GEORGE BLANDA**

with MICKEY HERSKOWITZ

Introduction by Dr. R. Graham Reedy

SIMON AND SCHUSTER
NEW YORK

Published by Simon and Schuster
A Division of Gulf & Western Corporation
Simon & Schuster Building
Rockefeller Center
1230 Avenue of the Americas
New York, New York 10020

Designed by Irving Perkins
Manufactured in the United States of America
1 2 3 4 5 6 7 8 9 10

Library of Congress Cataloging in Publication Data

Blanda, George, date.
Over forty: feeling great and looking good!
1. Middle aged men—Health and hygiene. 2 Blanda,
George, date.   3. Football players—United States—
Biography.   I. Herskowitz, Mickey, joint author.
II. Title.
RA777.8.B58   613'.04'37   78-1479

ISBN 0-671-22472-7

PHOTOGRAPHS BY BRUNO NOVER

TO BETTY, LESLIE AND GEORGE, JR.—
THREE GOOD REASONS FOR STAYING FIT.

For their sharing of time and information, the author wishes to thank Dr. Reginald Cherry of the Woodlands Clinic in Houston, George Anderson, trainer, Oakland Raiders, and Annie Housman, exercise physiologist.

Contents

Introduction

The first time I examined George Blanda, in the summer of 1971, he was forty-three—even then older than anyone who ever played pro football; older than his coach, older than the team doctor. But, physically, Blanda could have passed for ten or fifteen years younger. If you had not known his age, you would have had to carbon-date his bones to find out.

That day was my first, officially, on the job as team physician for the Oakland Raiders. A photographer snapped a picture of us—me in my blue smock, George in a towel. I soon discovered that he was the same in private—and you can't get much more private than a physical exam—as he came across on the football field. He was businesslike, self-assured, concentrating on whatever was in front of him.

Some athletes take a physical as though they were being interrogated by the Gestapo. Others seem to think they are in a canoe and you have to keep waking them. But Blanda observed every move I made and he talked easily, proudly, of how he had prepared for training camp. Eight weeks before, he had started running up to six miles a day. After he turned forty, he added a mile each year to his routine. The key to Blanda's career, to his record of endurance, was the fact that he knew his body and its limits. With the passage of time—once he became solely a place kicker—he ate less and trained longer. He knew his body would not respond as quickly as in his full contact days. George has often joked that he owed his survival to his ability to get out of bounds quickly. But no one ever questioned his toughness. He played linebacker one year in college, and again in his early seasons with the Chicago Bears.

"When I was young," he told me, "I could go to camp out of shape and in three weeks I'd be in condition. As I got older I had to be in shape when I got there." That summer we met, he had played handball, tennis and golf nearly every day in the off season. When he said he was ready to play, I had no reason to disbelieve him.

Blanda's enthusiasm was never forced. It was a necessary part of the formula he had developed for his own good physical health. It was a critical factor in his longevity as a pro football player. He was a fanatic about keeping his legs in shape. But he made his body obey his mind.

As I worked more and more with the Oakland Raiders, I saw many cases where a lesser player won a starting job away from a rival who had more talent, but who was lazy in his approach to fitness. In the classroom, in business, in life, the same kind of competition applies.

In these pages, Blanda offers some straight talk, long overdue, about a series of concepts in which he has come to believe and medical science supports. He also dispels a few myths. Ah, the many myths of exercise. Here are a few.

Exercise is (check one): fulfilling; life-prolonging; bad for your legs and back; harmful for the old; not recommended for girls, who will develop muscles and sagging breasts; suitable only to those who like the vigorous life; a guarantee against heart attacks; all of these. Actually, you can find books, pamphlets and articles in various journals that agree with nearly every one of the above statements.

So why, you have every reason to ask, another book on physical fitness? And why one by George Blanda? Simple. People can relate to Blanda. They saw what he was able to do, and how often he did it, well into his forties. They were reminded incessantly of his age, a reference that encouraged an entire generation, even as it agitated George. Anyone foolish enough to refer to him in person as "ol' George" is likely to get in return a look that would exterminate head lice.

But in 1970 Blanda became a hero to what has been called the Geritol Generation. He was the idol of the support-hose set. One syndicated columnist, Erma Bombeck, wrote that her husband kicked his tonic bottle thirty-two feet after one of George's game-winning field goals. That season he came off the bench to bring the Raiders from behind in four different games, with his arm and foot, to save them from defeat.

You can't take a nine-to-five clerk and apply to him the kind of physical conditioning a pro athlete needs. But he can surely draw some pointers, and some inspiration, from a fellow who played the toughest game of all until he was nearly forty-nine.

Knowing Blanda, I can promise the reader this: you needn't be a doctor to understand his message, and you needn't be a pro athlete to follow his suggestions.

Most of you out there reading this book are like me— lovers of sports, possibly several, but amateurs at doing them. Even those who can play more than one at a professional level will still be amateurs at the rest. Therefore, as we play less frequently, we become less "grooved." In this circumstance, we must all learn to get ourselves out of trouble when playing these games. Often I find myself— as in tennis and golf—with my weight on the back foot, flailing away at the ball or jumping too late, as in basketball; committing myself too soon in sandlot football. This then requires you and me to make sudden or unusual adjustments, often not even required by those who are experts in a particular sport. Therefore, you and I must be more flexible, have greater endurance and more patience than the pros, to accommodate our lack of skill.

In a sense, George Blanda has made this adjustment. His career ought to serve as a model for many of us. In many ways he has been fortunate. He outlasted most of his critics. And he never lost his independence. When George and I first considered the need for this kind of book, he insisted on two conditions: (1) that the information be medically sound, and (2) that it not contain any advice he doesn't believe or hasn't tried.

George is nothing if not consistent. He would never endorse a product he didn't use. He filmed commercials for the breakfast food he eats every morning, the aftershave lotion he always used, a truck he knew and drove during his years with a Chicago shipping firm, and Grecian Formula, the hair dye. In his TV commercial, Blanda smiles when he says, "I even leave a little gray in my sideburns." His friends find a twist of humor in the fact that George made some money out of growing older. But he turned down the advertising people who wanted him to say he smoked their cigarettes, or drank their soda, or sprinkled their foot powder between his toes. "I can't accept money for saying I like something I never use," he said. "There has to be some integrity in a person's life or nothing works very well very long."

Blanda and pro football worked together very well, for a very long time. "I just liked the game," George says. "I loved the routine. People say that football meetings and game films are boring. Not for me. I liked doing calisthenics. I liked the action on the sidelines. I liked being with other football players. . . . I could have quit a dozen times. I damned near did. Betty, my wife, had been wanting me to get out since 1959, the year the Bears let me go. My wife used to call my career 'Death and Resurrection.'"

Coincidentally, George and I left the Oakland Raiders in the same year, 1976, the year they went on to win the Super Bowl. I left to establish my own practice in a town called Enumclaw, Washington. Blanda went back to his home near Chicago to pursue new interests, and to enjoy a leisure he had never known before. He had begun his career with the Bears in the 1940s, continued through the fifties and sixties and into the seventies. Four decades. How he had winked at the calendar.

Leaving wasn't what George Blanda did best. Providing leadership, setting an example, rallying a team, this was where he excelled. He had the self-discipline of a U-boat commander. Still has.

Sports and medicine are natural allies. The games we

play are a good testing ground for ideas and techniques. George has already done it. Now we can let him show us how to look good and feel great.

R. GRAHAM REEDY
Team Physician (1971–76)
Oakland Raiders

First the Legs Go

It is always in season for old men to learn.
—AESCHYLUS

For most of my pro football career, and especially after I got past forty, I kept in shape between seasons with a regular program of running and cycling, plus handball or racquet ball. I did this more or less by instinct, and also out of my personal conviction that if I kept my legs in top shape the rest of me would do all right.

I remember the first time I met Dr. Graham Reedy, when he became team physician for the Oakland Raiders and was giving me a physical examination at the start of training camp. Half kidding, I offered to tell him the secret of it all: "Doc, it's my legs that keep me going—always the legs. Keep the legs in good shape and you'll always have the answer."

Dr. Reedy didn't bother to ask what the question was. He just cocked his head at me and went on with the exam. I suppose the "answer" I had in mind was the one for those

17

who wanted to know how an over-forty guy by the name of Blanda could still cut it in the NFL. I was used mostly as a place kicker in those later years, but don't you ever forget in my last NFL game, in the forty-eighth year of Blanda, he performed long enough at quarterback to throw a touchdown pass.

The point about my remarks that day to Dr. Reedy: *I was telling* him!

As I said, I had done my pre-camp conditioning instinctively, because I thought I knew better than anyone else what made the Blanda machine go. The program was designed to lengthen my pro football career. It so happened, what I had been doing for years was also a program designed for a more important goal: *to lengthen my life.*

That's the reason this book has come to be written. *Not* to illustrate how a guy over forty kept coming back every year in the NFL, but to show how the average person, male or female, can follow a reasonable program of exercise which can lengthen the life span, and spend those additional years looking good and feeling great.

This is a story of practical results—through the sum of my own experiences—backed up by physiological science, gathered together by Dr. Reedy from his own background in sports medicine.

This is not a book about how to diet and lose weight. But you will no doubt achieve substantial weight loss along the way.

This is not a book prescribing a program of hard exercise with multiple repetitions, the kind of workout that would leave you breathless quickly. In fact, that kind of exercise is dangerous, even to some young men. But, when you have achieved the goals of *your own* program, your body will be capable of such short bursts of energy without any threatening results.

The bedrock of this book is what some people regard as a "new science," the relationship of healthy lungs and a healthy cardiovascular system in terms of a long life. "Cardio" refers to the heart, and "vascular" to the blood-vessel system. Of course, it is not "new" at all. It is simply better publicized now, so that the whole subject is better known to laymen.

The average informed person now says, "Yeah, cardiovascular. I want some of that!"

Well, that's basically what this book is about.

As long ago as the Korean War, it was evident the American way of life was not the healthiest in the world. Autopsies performed on our soldiers produced startling results. They showed a 40 percent blockage of two of the four major blood vessels of the heart—*at age twenty-one!*

Primitive man, even a hundred years ago, led a life mainly of physical work. Modern man leads a life in which he relies on his mind and his skills. That's particularly true in America, but even in some of the hardier countries there was similar evidence.

A man named Karvonen in Finland did a study comparing that country's championship skiers to the average male population. He found that among the average males 50 percent were alive at age sixty-five. Among the skiers, 50 percent were alive at age seventy-two. At ninety, 10 percent of the skiers were still living, but only 2 percent of the others.

Studies such as these long ago convinced much of the

medical profession that *certain types of exercises,* which helped increase the efficiency of the cardiovascular system, would lead directly to longer lives.

Your heart rate, the beat of your pulse, should be 50 to 70 per minute when the body is at rest. If it is significantly higher than that, the body is probably in poor general condition. A regular program of exercise—the long, slow, steady kind of exercise—can reduce the heartbeat from 70 to 50 or even 40. It doesn't take a math major to figure out that in a drop from 70 to 50 the heartbeats saved during the waking hours are substantial. Over the year, the heart would have a net "vacation" of three and a half months.

What I have been emphasizing here is the bottom line: those added years watching sunsets and sunrises and your grandchildren toddling into your arms.

But there are plenty other bonuses along the way. I'll borrow a phrase that has become very popular lately: the quality of life. Dr. Reedy tells me that people who continue to keep up a regular program of exercise (he calls this the "compliance" factor), when asked why they stay with it, invariably answer along these lines: "I do it because it makes me feel better. Because it makes me think more clearly. It relieves the tensions that used to bug me. I also do believe I'm more creative in my thinking, because I feel fresh and alert at work now, instead of logy and draggy."

Regular exercise is some kind of natural high! Be warned: If you continue it long enough, you'll be hooked for life. That's what I call a very healthy addiction.

There is an additional bonus from a regular program of exercise: the way it affects your personal appearance. I'm not referring to the splendor of physique, the trim-hipped miler, the slat-bellied Olympic swimmer, the ripple-muscled championship boxer. I am referring to what happens when a pair of healthy lungs, uncluttered by smoke and coaxed to near-capacity several times a week, feed oxygen from the atmosphere into the heart, and the heart circulates blood to every part of the body. The result is a special glow in the skin tone, a sparkle in clear eyes, a lively spring in the step. *Looking good!*

Dr. Reedy once embarrassed me by stating, "Few men at thirty-five compare to Blanda in our culture." I won't quibble at a compliment, but I will say I sure as hell don't feel like forty-nine, and regular exercise has everything to do with it. I've always felt that age was only a number. Age is attitude. I've known people in their seventies who still had *potential*. And I've known guys in their thirties who were fat and sloppy and over the hill.

Finally, there is one surefire bonus derived from regular exercise, unknown to people who haven't tried it: *Exercise is its own guarantee of success.*

For example, if a husband and wife decide to begin their exercise program by walking two miles every other night, at the beginning it might take them forty-five minutes to complete the distance. That is a pace hardly more than a stroll. But after repeated two-mile tours, they will find their walking time is down to forty-two minutes, then thirty-eight—with no discomfort. In time the couple will be walking two miles in a flat thirty minutes, and that is breezing briskly along. And they will be enjoying it.

This built-in progress is just another wonder of the human body. Doctors of sports medicine refer to this as the "training effect"—which means that when the body is asked to do greater than normal work, it responds by increasing its ability to do more work. The more the body is asked to do, exercise, the better its ability to respond to sudden stress and other work in general.

Just as there are automatic bonuses that result from a regular exercise program, there are many myths about exercise that discourage the average person from even beginning.

The two major misconceptions are: (1) To burn up the number of calories equal to one pound of fat, a man would have to walk for thirty-six hours, split wood for seven hours, or play volleyball for eleven hours; in other words, hopeless. (2) Exercise makes you hungry; hunger makes you eat more; therefore, you will gain more weight because of exercise than you will lose.

Dr. Jean Mayer has destroyed both of these myths. Dr. Mayer, a Harvard nutritionist, is today president of Tufts University.

Again, this is not a book dealing primarily with weight loss, but that subject is a powerful motivating force for most people who are contemplating an exercise program, and I'll take motivation anywhere I can get it.

First the "hopeless" charge. "The implication," points out Dr. Mayer,

is that the exercise is done at one stretch. Actually, of course, the cost of splitting wood for seven hours will be equivalent to one pound of fat even though the seven hours may not constitute one stretch. Thus, while splitting wood for seven consecutive hours would be difficult for anyone other than a Paul Bunyan, splitting wood for one half hour every day, by no means an impossible task for a healthy man, would add up to seven hours in a fortnight. If it represented a *regular* practice [italics mine], it would by the very reasoning of detractors of exercise represent the caloric equivalent of 26 pounds of body fat in a year. A half hour of handball or squash a day would be equivalent to 16 pounds in a year.*

The second myth, that exercise creates a hungry man, is appealing: "I worked so hard today, I could eat a horse!" Yes, but that's not exactly what happens. An increase in activity, Dr. Mayer proved in experiments with Harvard student volunteers, is followed by an increase in food intake *only within a range of normal activity*. On a program of vigorous exercise, beyond the range of normal activity, food intake actually *decreases*.

The other side of the coin causes all the trouble in the first place. A decrease in activity is followed by a decrease in food ("When I was a kid I really used to put away the groceries, but now I don't have an appetite and I still get fatter"). That's why, in the sedentary life of the average man, the decrease in activity overtakes the decrease in food intake, resulting in obesity. Dr. Mayer pointed out that farmers have known this for centuries, as indicated in their practice of penning up cattle, hogs and geese for fattening. The animals grow fat because they are denied room to exercise.

I am convinced [concluded Dr. Mayer] that inactivity is the most important factor explaining the frequency of 'creeping' overweight in modern Western societies. The regulation of food intake was never designed to adapt to the highly mechanized sedentary conditions of modern life, any more than animals were meant to be caged. Adaptation to these conditions without development of obesity means that either

*From a paper, "Exercise and Weight Control," presented by Dr. Mayer to a symposium at the University of Illinois.

the individual will have to step up his activity or that he will be mildly or acutely hungry all his life.

All my pro football career I had to battle that "creeping" overweight problem Dr. Mayer mentions, and it wasn't so darned creeping. More like galloping in the off season. But now my career is over and there is the far more important reason to continue a program of regular exercise.

The fact is, the majority of all Americans die of heart disease. Think about that for a moment. Heart disease is our number-one killer. Another stunning statistic is that in 55 percent of heart attacks the first "symptom" is the sudden death of the victim. No second chances there, my friend, no program of recuperative treatment. Out of the blue it hits them, and—gone.

But, thankfully, our approach to health in this country is undergoing a radical change right now. Before, when I was kicking field goals for the Raiders and occasionally throwing a touchdown pass, I never concerned myself with the subject. After completing my on-field career, and as a result of many conversations with Dr. Reedy, I have made it my business to keep up with what is going on. I'm in a bigger Game right now, the game of survival, and I intend to be a winner there, for as long as I possibly can.

Part of the change is centered around the type of medicine being practiced. For centuries doctors have been trying to treat disease. They are trained to recognize disease, diagnose it and prescribe for it, and treat it. And yet in the case of heart disease this simply doesn't work.

For example, not long ago we spent $50 million a year on heart-bypass surgery, rerouting the flow of blood from a damaged artery to a still-healthy one. All our big guns were saved to treat the disease after it had already taken effect. That's where most of the money went, to Dr. Michael De Bakey and the Texas Heart Institute, which was good. But they were getting the patient fifteen or so years after the disease had taken hold. Finally, people began to realize the money should have been directed a different way, much earlier.

When Baylor Medical Hospital was celebrating De Bakey's twenty-seventh year, the doctor's message was, "We have got to have a new approach to preventive medicine." In 1976 when he had a conference for physicists, presumably to talk about his transplants and a mechanical heart, over half the questions from the audience were about diet, and exercise, and prevention.

In essence, that's what this book is about—a sort of preventive medicine, a way to chart your own program of exercise and achieve cardiovascular health.

I promise you, you will be surprised at how easy it is, and doubly surprised at the almost instant rewards.

As I said, I staggered into this whole area more or less by accident, simply because I wanted to keep my legs in shape. I always remembered the wisecrack of Willie Pep, the great featherweight champion. Willie said, "First the legs go, then your reflexes go, then your friends go."

I'm not that cynical. I have a lot of best friends, beginning with my family, and I intend to stay around a long time to enjoy them.

CHAPTER II

The Self-Starter

In a scene from the hottest motion picture of 1976, *Rocky*, a half-punchy club fighter begins his roadwork for a bout with the heavyweight champion of the world. The morning sky is still dark as tar. We see him wheezing as he drags himself up the steps of the Philadelphia Museum of Art.

But if you believe in dreams, you knew what was going to happen: by the time the improbable fight drew near he would be soaring, taking the steps three at a time and throwing his arms in the air at the top as the music swells.

Do you remember the last time—any time—that you succeeded at some physical task, and came away with that fly-like-an-eagle feeling? Great, wasn't it?

Rocky had a goal. He didn't expect to win. He knew he couldn't beat the champion. But he wanted to go the distance, to last the full fifteen rounds, and prove he wasn't "just another bum from the neighborhood."

We all need goals. They give us a sense of our own worth. During my last ten years in pro football, I had a ritual. Starting about six weeks before training camp, I would run every day, two miles, four, or six, getting my legs—and the rest of me—in shape. My "track" was at the West Suburban YMCA in La Grange, Illinois, where I make my home, outside Chicago. A beaten path around the baseball field winds for half a mile, and on any given day a dozen or more joggers will be out there, pounding away. We have a fairly determined group, people who are concerned about their health and the way they look. A few of them enter the Boston Marathon each year.

There is a fringe benefit to jogging or running. Your mind is free to consider ideas you might not have time for otherwise. A runner is alone with his thoughts, and you *need* them. It is important to let your mind wander, so that you won't be thinking about the pounding your feet and body are taking. I always used those moments to get myself psyched up. With each stride I would tell myself, "If you don't run you're not going to make the team . . . you're not going to have all that excitement . . . you won't be out there with the Oakland Raiders. . . . If you quit now someone else will take your job . . . you'll lose the thing you love."

Sure, exercise can be painful or boring or both. But what you have to know is that it will lead to something better down the line. I'm out of football now, as of the 1976 season. Someone did take my job (it was *given* to him, actually). But it wasn't because I lost my motivation. I still run, jog, ride a bicycle, play handball, tone my muscles. Keeping fit has been a part of me for so long now I can't stop. It is my addiction. I would never give my critics the satisfaction of seeing me get sloppy.

I have never really gotten very far from my roots, from my boyhood in Youngwood, Pennsylvania. I was a tough, competitive Slavic kid struggling—always—to avoid the dust of the mines. Youngwood was known as a railroad and steel mill town, but around the area other men, including my father, earned hard dollars digging for coal. They worked below the ground all week, swinging a pick, and you saw them on the week end, which was drinking time. We had a warm house and serviceable clothes and we had food. But if my father made more than two thousand dollars it was one hell of a year. But I never thought we were poor.

As a boy I was chubby, running to fat. I grew up on starches. Our basic diet included lots of potatoes and bread. We'd burn off the calories at the football field a block from my house. I had six brothers, three older and three younger, and all of us played. We'd go over to the field and we'd play whatever was in season. Football, basketball, baseball, track. We would cut branches off the trees and play street hockey. That was how we entertained ourselves. We couldn't afford bicycles.

So I was always active and always in shape, and sports became a way of life. If you grew up in Youngwood you were expected to try out for football and play on a winning team. That area turned out some great athletes. From within a range of twenty-five miles of where I lived came Arnold Palmer, Stan Musial, Johnny Lujack, John Unitas, Chuck Knox and Bill George.

I knew if I wanted to go to college, and improve myself, and stay the hell out of the mines, I had to do it through athletics. My dad couldn't afford to send us. I have a vivid memory of my childhood years, of fellows from my home town going off to college, and within a year they would be out of school and back home, for one reason or another. It always struck me that they were quitters. They couldn't stick it out. I made up my mind that if I went to college I was going to play football and graduate and there was no way I was going to be embarrassed back home.

That idea was what motivated me at the University of Kentucky. It was all I thought about when school turned hard and I encountered a football coach named Paul (Bear) Bryant, who practiced the team for eleven months. I wanted to quit, and then I told myself, "No, I can't. I'm not going home and face those people without playing football and getting a degree."

I was never a fanatic about physical fitness, but I can honestly say I learned from someone who was. I had finished my freshman season at Kentucky on a team that went one-and-nine when Coach Bryant was brought in from Maryland. My first impression of him when he arrived on the campus was, "This must be what God looks like." He was big and smooth and handsome, with a voice that rumbled out of his throat like a train out of a tunnel. His first year we really did work out for eleven months. I don't know if that was legal, but you could get away with it. Coach Bryant would scrimmage us in the late summer heat for two or three hours, and then everyone who was still alive had to go through another hour of special drills.

The year was 1946, right after the war, and we had this combination of returning veterans who had fought their way across oceans and raw kids who had played as freshmen and sophomores. And Coach Bryant had people coming in from all over the country. He had coached at Bain-bridge Naval Station, in Maryland, and he knew where every stray athlete in America was hiding. We must have had five hundred kids come through Lexington on tryouts. It was survival of the fittest, all right. It was like the old joke about having three teams—one playing, one coming and one going.

He worked our fannies off. We had a spring practice, a summer practice, an early-fall practice. He didn't allow us to smoke, drink, curse or carry on with girls. If he saw us with one he'd tell us, "Enjoy how warm and soft that little hand you're holding is, because the memory of it is going to keep you company on the bench this Saturday."

But above all, Bear Bryant motivated us. He taught me discipline, respect and dedication. I owe the length of my career to him and to his coaching philosophy: hard work equals success. I didn't like the system at first. I wanted to be a goof-off like everyone else. But you could see he got results. We won seven games his first year and eight the next. He convinced me that hard work would get you someplace. Bryant laid the groundwork for my whole life.

If you had any dog in you, the Bear would find it. If you had a tendency to quit, you would have quit under Coach Bryant. And I can tell you, the best time not to quit is the first time. It gets easier after that.

Of course, by the time you are over forty you are not likely to be taking orders from your college football coach. So you have to reach down inside you and tap whatever pride is there. When you get right down to it, you have to motivate yourself.

Coaches have been known to go to remarkable lengths to light a fire under a player, to instill in him the so-called "killer instinct." In his early years with the New York Giants, Rosey Grier became a special project of his coach, Jim Lee Howell, who didn't think Rosey was mean enough. "You've got to *punish* your man to make him respect you." Howell would say, and then he'd wince when Grier would help an opposing quarterback to his feet.

Howell finally gave up on his Grier campaign after the incident of the Published Scouting Report. Unnoticed by Howell, two writers were present when the defense was given a belittling rundown of the next opponent, Philadelphia. This Eagle was "too slow to cover the sweep," another would "quit if you take him on physically." The comments made great reading in the next day's sports pages and even better reading when picked up by the papers in Philadelphia. At a team meeting, Howell sought to turn the situation around. "Those guys have been reading this stuff all week," he said. "They're going to come in here Sunday with fire in their eyes, spoiling for blood. So—what are *we* going to do about it?" Howell happened to be looking at Grier when he roared the question, and Rosey jumped up and said, "Maybe it isn't too late—we could wire them an apology."

It took time, but the gentle Rosey Grier learned to motivate himself and became one of the great tackles in the NFL. Unfortunately for the Giants, by then he was with the Los Angeles Rams.

The point is that no one can force you to take care of yourself. The doctor can show the charts, quote the tables and call a red alert. Your wife can nag. And you can talk all you want about starting a program. But exercising your mouth won't help your cardiovascular system.

Some people are born with a competitive spirit. When an interviewer once asked my wife what I was really like, Betty replied that when our daughter, Leslie, was little and her friends came over to jump rope, they would never ask me to join them because they figured I would try to win. Well, hell yes.

Why should so many of us need to be *persuaded* to improve our health, feel better and look sharper? The incentives for doing so are all around us. Maybe there is someone at the office you are competing against, or a person whose opinion you want to raise, or whose encouragement you need to justify. If you don't like what you see in the mirror in the morning, what better reason to get in shape?

One way or another, your health affects your pocketbook. Medical bills can be avoided. Your ability to work or think or study will be enhanced. And often the effect is direct and immediate.

When I broke in with the Chicago Bears, George Halas, the coach, assigned a set weight to each player—usually whatever you weighed when you got out of college. If you played ten years you had to maintain that same weight. An incredible system, but no one questioned it. In those days you didn't question anything. During the season we weighed in every Wednesday, and you were fined fifty dollars for every extra pound. Now, this was well before the boom in pro football salaries. As a rule they paid you enough to keep you from gnawing on the furniture. So a fifty-dollar fine was not taken lightly.

The night before the weigh-in the players would go to

the steam baths, gulp down Ex-Lax or water pills, just anything. I can remember standing under a hot shower for two
hours, running in place, trying to shed four pounds, so I
would not have to cough up that two hundred dollars.

All of which is by way of explaining a little of George
Blanda to you. No, this is not a football book, but it helps
to know where a fellow came from. I believe you can
apply the lessons I have learned, in certain cases by knowing what not to do. One other point needs to be made, for
the record. I thought I could still play football when the
Raiders let me go. I still think so. I did not go gladly. But
I'm not bitter and I have no regrets. My feelings about the
game are clear. Football enabled me to make something
out of my life. It got me through high school and college,
and led to a good job with a trucking firm, and later commercials and endorsements.

I owe everything to professional football. I have no com-
plaints. No one ever forced me to play football on any level
(and I am opposed to *any* parent forcing *any* child to compete against his or her will). I never felt dehumanized. To
the contrary, football is a humanizing experience. You
meet people of different social backgrounds, different na-
tionalities and races, and you wind up with one goal. To
succeed. Or survive.

There are no shortcuts to the top. I learned that from
Bear Bryant, and it applies as much to your own health as
to winning football games. I can only tell you that whatever your motivation—money, pride, love or the influence
of someone you respect (or fear)—the price will be worth
it. You will see and feel the difference in the most elemental
ways. To begin with, if you exercise properly you will sleep

better. As for myself, I need those eight hours (most athletes tend to be lazy, anyway). Not everyone requires that much sleep, but I think it is important to give your body a chance to recuperate. You'll feel less cranky. You'll think less about yesterday and more about tomorrow.

Exercise is like education. It goes on every day of your life. The idea is to get as much as you can, just short of pain.

CHAPTER III

The Heart Is Already in It

In the medical definition of "fitness" there are five points:

1. Endurance, stamina.

2. Flexibility. The muscles and joints are able to move with ease.

3. Strength.

4. Relaxation, the ability to put the body at ease.

5. Coordination, putting all of the above together, as in developing a good game of tennis.

Of these five points, Number 1 is by far the most important, because it's through an increase in endurance and stamina that the lungs and the heart and the blood vessels are involved in a most healthy way.

From this new focus on the lungs and the cardiovascular system, many doctors have become interested in an approach to exercise which is now called "aerobics," made popular by Dr. Kenneth Cooper.

Aerobics simply means exercise which uses oxygen at low enough levels to draw it from the outside atmosphere and not from our body stores. Typical aerobic exercises are walking, jogging, cycling, swimming, rowing—activities that you can do continuously for fifteen to thirty minutes without stopping.

"Continuously" is a key word in aerobics. A stop-and-start, pause-and-rest sequence undoes all you're trying to do. Even on a two-mile walking program, when you have to stop for a stoplight you are losing some of the benefits of the whole exercise.

The goal in aerobic exercise is to increase your heart rate to a level of 70 to 85 percent of your greatest capacity. Normally, your maximum heart rate is your age subtracted from 220. If you're forty, then the maximum rate is 180. So to hit 70 to 85 percent of that, you should do enough exercise to bring your pulse within the range of 126 to 153 beats per minute.

This is a whole different ball game from the old ideas of body building and physical fitness, such as the Charles Atlas series that equipped a skinny guy to bop the guy that kicked sand in his face. Weight-lifting, sprinting, all types of calisthenics that make you breathless quickly, are what the medical profession always calls "anaerobics." A program of such exercises is frowned on, because the body is forced to use oxygen from its own system, rather than from the outside. They put a quick load on the heart and the lungs, and a whole lot of studies have been made showing that there is very little beneficial effect over the long haul.

Doctors more and more are prescribing the long, slow and long-distance elements of aerobic exercise for their patients. Again, this is a fairly new development. Among my friends outside of sports, I've heard a hundred times or more "I don't feel good. In fact, I feel lousy. But I just had a checkup and the doc said there wasn't a thing wrong with me." Sometimes these guys who don't have a thing wrong with them drop dead at a church dance the following Saturday night.

Doctors had for so long been taught about disease deterioration, they rarely looked at "health" from any standpoint except the absence of disease. Now they are beginning to look at the subtleties of "poor health." They are realizing that being fat and sedentary can cause a tremendous amount of poor health among their patients who have "nothing wrong" with them.

They are prescribing slow, gradual and lengthening programs of exercise for these people, to help them escape the scary threat of sudden death from coronary disease. Dr. Kenneth Cooper, the aerobic expert, tells a story about a Houston stewardess who had to learn CPR—cardiopulmonary resuscitation procedures—before she could qualify with her airline. It seems that in the six months prior to her hiring, five people had sustained heart attacks rushing to the ticket counter. They had parked their cars a hundred yards away, grabbed a heavy suitcase, and hurried to make their flight. It is very likely that had any of those people been on a constant regular program of continuous mild exercise, their hearts would have been able to stand the strain of a sudden surge in energy.

On the other hand, many people find an excuse to avoid exercise, of any kind, by pointing to news stories about jogging deaths, or the deaths of professional athletes. The very fact that these stories make little headlines all over the country shows that they fall in the "man bites dog" category.

A few years ago wide receiver Chuck Hughes of the Detroit Lions died on the football field during a Sunday game. Physicians from both teams tried in vain to revive him. Later an autopsy showed that his blood vessels had become almost entirely blocked with cholesterol plaques, a condition that his physical exam hadn't discovered. (In the next chapter I'll outline the series of tests you should have before starting to exercise.) The Chuck Hughes case was simply a medical rarity. Later, Hughes's young son was checked and found to have very high blood fat levels *at age seven!*

In California, two joggers died of heart attacks on the same day. More headlines. It turned out that both were victims of severe heart trouble, and one had been ordered by his doctor to do no exercise at all.

More numerous, and documented, are the heart specialists who brought their patients back to full health with a carefully prescribed exercise program. In 1972 a Massachusetts cardiologist and eight of his patients who had had heart attacks ran in the Boston Marathon—26 miles, 385 yards. Seven of the eight men completed the distance in just over four hours.

Until recently a heart attack relegated the victim to the life of a semi-invalid. If he was wealthy he installed an elevator in his home to dodge the stairs; a ramp replaced the front steps. If he was poor he retired from work, settled into a rocking chair on the front porch and swatted flies— gently. Family relatives kicked in for the groceries.

Some lay groups were among the first to reverse this idea. The Cleveland YMCA's Cardiac Club is now famous.

It began when a doctor told municipal executive William Rogers that he should take exercise. Rogers had just suffered the second of two heart attacks, twenty years apart. William Cumler, physical director of the YMCA, put Rogers on a gradually increasing schedule of jogging, swimming and light calisthenics. Rogers' very first step was to walk back and forth across the swimming pool in chest-high water. At the end of the program, Rogers was jogging a mile, swimming a mile and doing a half hour of calisthenics—all of this every day.

This subject of fatal heart attacks is very personal to me, because of Oakland quarterback Ken Stabler. I like to think Ken is a protégé of mine. He was young enough and cocky enough not to feel threatened by this old pro. We played golf together frequently. In the summer of 1970, Ken's father dropped dead of a heart attack in Birmingham. He was forty-six, three years older than I.

More people are now beginning to ask, even demand, that their doctors prescribe a definite exercise program for them. In some ways, Americans are programmed people. They are comfortable with instructions that specify so many hours and so many days a week. People are now telling their doctors, "Look, you prescribed penicillin for me, you told me to take four tablets a day for ten days and then come back and see you. I want the same thing for exercise. I don't want you to give me a bottle of tablets and tell me to take one when I feel like it."

Haphazard exercise—usually the anaerobic varieties of exercise—is not the answer. I gave a talk to a group not long ago in which I suggested that more people ought to get into a regular program of exercise, such as I'm outlining in this book. A lady raised her hand and said, "Many of my friends are square dancers, they play tennis, they have swimming pools in their back yards, and they're all having heart attacks. You're telling us that exercise is good for you?"

I tried to explain. Our concept of exercise—until the studies in aerobics—missed the whole point. What is needed is a plan of exercise for developing the heart muscle. Just because a person sweats, and his heart rate increases, does not mean he is getting any cardiovascular benefit.

Think about it. Take the corner butcher, who chops meat all day. Physically he is working very hard and physically he's very tired at the end of the day. And yet he is just as liable to have a heart attack as someone who does nothing. Why is that? It's because the butcher is not benefiting from cardiovascular exercise. The medical profession now has the means to prescribe for that. The exercise stress test consists of walking on a moving belt, or sitting on a stationary bike, and exercising while your heart is being monitored. When one can no longer continue, the maximal pulse rate is established. To attain a training effect, a prescription is based on 60 to 85 percent of that level. Then people can square dance, play tennis, whatever gives them pleasure—but they'll also have a basic program that will give them a margin of safety.

According to national polls on the subject, 20 percent of the population does not care one hoot about exercise. They will never exercise, literally, for love or money. Another 20 percent does actively exercise. The other 60 percent in between wants to, or is willing to get on a program, but can't quite make up its mind. So this book is written for that 60 percent that wants to and will exercise, with a little push from their friends.

It shouldn't take that much of a push. We are talking about three to four times a week (a day of rest between sessions) at twenty to thirty to forty-five minutes a whack, depending upon the exercise plan you select. At the maximum, that's a program of two hours and forty minutes per week—out of your 112 waking hours. In most cases it will be the equivalent of missing one late movie a week.

The normal result is that within eight weeks of gradually increasing your capacity for distance within a certain time, you will begin getting the optimum benefit for your heart and lungs. The heart beats more slowly. The lungs expand more easily.

A side bonus is that you will begin to feel more alert mentally. Chess has to be the most mind-sapping exercise we know of, particularly when played at the top international level. Do you know how Bobby Fischer and Boris Spassky prepared for their great showdown in Iceland? They swam, they jogged, they played their favorite sports. They were well aware that a healthy and well-conditioned body clears the cobwebs from the brain.

The least demanding exercise, I will suggest to you in the next chapter, is walking, and yet walking is the one exercise in which strain and fatigue are reduced to a minimum while at the same time giving virtually every part of the body a workout. Energy expended in a five-mile walk at a steady three-miles-an-hour pace is definitely more valuable than that expended by a top tennis player in three fast sets of singles.

A caution about some things that *won't* do you any good: saunas, steam baths, mineral baths and the idea that anything that makes you sweat helps you get fit. It's just not so. It may feel good by relaxing the body, but that's all.

Also forget the expensive motorized machines that are supposed to get you in condition with the motor doing most of the work—stationary bicycles plugged into a wall socket, the wooden whirligigs guaranteed to roll away your fat. There is no such shortcut. A girl asked Dr. Cooper at his Aerobic Center in Dallas how many points she got from horseback riding. Cooper said, "None. The horse gets them all."

The key to conditioning your heart and lungs is my oft-stated premise that your heart rate must be pulsing at 60 to 85 percent of capacity. After you have found what that rate is, you will have to learn how to check yourself to be sure your amount of effort is reaching that goal.

The problem is that your body will steadily improve as you continue to exercise. If you start out walking two miles a day in forty-five minutes, pretty soon you will be whipping the distance in forty minutes, then thirty-eight, and on down to thirty. By this time your body is so proficient the two-mile distance probably will not have your heart rate operating at the 60-to-85 percent level. The answer is to spend the forty-five minutes walking *three* miles.

How will you know this? You will have to learn to count your own heart rate. I always figured this was a professional mystery known only to nurses and other professionals. But it turns out to be not that difficult. The first time I tried to take my pulse at the wrist I decided I was a dead man. There was nothing there.

Fortunately, there is an easy way to do this. Use the carotid artery on either side of your neck. Feel for the angle of the jaw and put your third finger directly beneath that angle. Push gently toward the windpipe until you can feel the throb of the pulse. Use the sweep-second on your watch as you count the pulsations for ten seconds. Multiply by six. This tells you your heart rate per minute. The idea behind using only the ten-second count and multiplying by six is that the first ten seconds after you complete your exercise program is the crucial figure.

There are a number of additional benefits to a program of continuous, slow and long-distance exercise. Among them is the fact that proper exercise can lower the blood-pressure count. A San Diego study showed that twenty minutes of calisthenics and thirty to thirty-five minutes of jogging, twice a week, reduced blood pressure by 8 *percent*.

I have just reread this chapter, and the thought suddenly struck me that I wish I hadn't had to write it. I wish everybody in the country knew all these things about exercise and the lungs and the heart, so that everybody was out there working to preserve his or her life. That's how vital this whole subject is.

CHAPTER IV

Pick Your Own Medicine

Now comes the moment of truth: how to select and start a program. I can anticipate your first objection. "Hey, I don't have all that much time. Anyway, why do I need a program when I have my weekend golf and tennis?"

No exercise is beneficial unless it is done properly. That is, with the right kind of effort, under the right conditions, in the right gear. Many a doctor sends his kids to college from the fees brought in by tennis elbows, shin splints, pulled hamstrings, sore ankles and dog bites suffered by weekend athletes. Or by those over forty who decide to regain their sophomore form in one afternoon.

And time? You have the rest of your life, if you work it right. All anyone needs is thirty to forty-five minutes, three or four times a week, to establish a program that will improve looks, shed pounds and add years. And reduce the risk of dropping dead from coronary heart disease, the nation's number-one killer.

The first step is to select one or more of the following exercises: jogging, bicycle riding, swimming, rowing, or walking (briskly). Any one, or a combination of these, will produce the results you want: build up the heart and the lungs, open up veins and arteries, and make illness far less likely to strike.

Pick an exercise tailored to your own needs and circumstance. If you live in a heavily trafficked area, obviously jogging might not be ideal. If you have a back-yard pool, swimming ought to be your ticket. If you are fortunate enough to live on a lake, and enjoy the water, try rowing. Never mind what Frank Howard, the folksy football coach at Clemson, once said when his athletic department was asked to sponsor a rowing team: "Clemson will never subsidize a sport in which a man sits on his ass and goes backward."

There is no reason why your choice can't be based at least in part on fun and convenience. But if you can stand the tedium, jogging is generally rated as the best of all aerobic conditioners. By comparison, if you jog a mile in eight minutes, that is equal to swimming twenty-four laps in fifteen minutes, or cycling five miles in twenty minutes, or playing handball for thirty-five minutes, or running in place for twelve and a half minutes.

Once you have in mind an exercise that you can and will attempt, you should consult a doctor, undergo a complete physical and ask for a stress test. If your doctor does not have a treadmill, a device designed for such tests, he can refer you to the nearest cardiovascular clinic. No one, regardless of his or her medical history, should undertake a program of physical activity without an examination.

The treadmill measures the heart's ability to do the work

while at its highest level of stress. The treadmill is like a motor-driven conveyor belt. A group of electrodes are placed on your chest and an electrocardiogram is evaluated while you walk, briskly. Dr. Reedy tells his patients to imagine that they are a grandparent watering the lawn or weeding the flowers in their own front yard while a grandchild is playing down the block. Suddenly, you hear the screeching of car brakes and you look up just in time to see that the child is yours, struck by the car. In effect, the treadmill measures what happens to your heart during the time you leave your front yard until you get to that grandchild's side. The object is to measure the heart and body under a great amount of physical stress. At the end of the test, the doctors are able to judge the level of your fitness and prescribe exercise accordingly.

Another aerobic test to define your fitness is called the twelve-minute run. The object is to run or walk, comfortably, as far as you can in twelve minutes. If you get winded you slow down until you catch your breath. Then you run again until your time is up. A chart prepared by Dr. Cooper explains the levels of fitness:

THE 12-MINUTE TEST
(Distances in miles covered in 12 minutes)

FITNESS	AGE			
CATEGORY	**Under 30**	**30–39**	**40–49**	**50 +**
I. Very poor	1.0	.95	.85	.80
II. Poor	1.0 –1.24	.95–1.14	.85–1.04	.80–.99
III. Fair	1.25–1.49	1.15–1.39	1.05–1.29	1.0 –1.24
IV. Good	1.50–1.74	1.40–1.64	1.30–1.54	1.25–1.49
V. Very Good	1.75+	1.65+	1.55+	1,50+

Aside from its scientific value, the treadmill can be easily adapted to a home training program. The unit is not widely used for two reasons: (1) it is expensive (a good unit for home use costs around $1,000), and (2) it is boring. Both factors can be offset to some degree. Doctors will write a prescription for one if the condition of the patient justifies its use. The equipment then becomes a perfectly legitimate tax deduction.

The boredom can be reduced by placing the treadmill in front of your television set. Ideally, most of us like to get our exercises over with in twenty minutes or so. You could get in your jogging as you watched *The Today Show,* in a constant temperature, without having to worry about the neighborhood hounds. It is really an ideal way to time yourself. You know when the show starts, when it ends, or at which commercial break you need to get off.

The machine can be adjusted to operate at speeds equivalent to walking or jogging, and to form an incline. A 5 percent constant incline is usually recommended, at a pace of three and a half to four miles an hour, for seventeen minutes.

Of course, there are simpler, less costly ways of achieving your purpose. A lot of people who need help the most are travelers. And here are two exercises that are surefire:

1. Jumping rope. Try it, you'll like it. Some people say they can't jump rope. Nonsense. Just jump a minute and half a day the first week. Anyone can jump rope unless he or she has some kind of malformation. You can start your program at eighty to ninety steps a minute and progress from there. It takes eight weeks to work up to the maximum, but the advantage is obvious. You can pack a rope in your suitcase and take it everywhere. It is literally a portable gym. Today they even make jump ropes with a five-pound weight built into the handle to exercise your

arms. You can do it for ten minutes, tire yourself out, and sleep like a baby.

2. Running in place. Obviously, this is the simplest exercise of all. But it is boring and can cause some ankle and knee problems, because your foot doesn't have a chance to bounce and the weight isn't distributed from the ball back to the heel, as it would normally. There are shoes that can simulate the effect of a grassy surface, however. It is also a good idea to buy a little piece of foam and carry a square of it in your suitcase. Running on foam will eliminate many of the problems. (It will also provide a cushion in the event you are carrying anything breakable in your bag.)

Do you have any idea how old an exercise running in place is? How about *circa* 400 B.C.? In one of Xenophon's lighthearted reports on life in Athens, Socrates was asked for the secret of his vitality. How was it that he stayed fresh in spirit and keen of wit, on into the conversational hours of the night?

"Because," said Socrates, "I dance every morning."

"It's true," a friend said. "I found him doing it and I thought he'd gone mad. But he talked to me and I tell you he convinced me. When I went home, I did not dance; I don't know how; but I waved my arms about."

Socrates lived to age seventy—in an era when people didn't live that long—and might be going yet, if he hadn't downed that cup of hemlock. So anything the old boy did to insure longevity is worth noting.

This is the time to note that there are some people who should *not* undertake a vigorous program for any reasons, at any time. The stress test will spot them, if the doctor hasn't. Dr. Reedy's list of these people would include:

1. Those with moderate to severe heart disease, who experience chest pain during minimal activity.

2. Recent heart attack victims. You must wait at least three months after an attack before starting a program; and then not without the clearance of your doctor and preferably under medical supervision.

3. Anyone with heart disease of the valves, primarily as a result of rheumatic fever. These patients should not exercise at all—not even to the extent of fast walking—without a doctor's clearance.

4. Certain types of congenital (at birth) heart disease cases, particularly those in which the surface of the body turns blue during exertion.

5. Those with enlarged hearts due to high blood pressure.

6. Those with severe irregularities of the heartbeat, requiring medication or frequent medical attention.

7. Those with uncontrolled diabetes from too much or not enough blood sugar.

8. Patients with high blood pressure exceeding 180 over 110 with medication.

9. Anyone with an infectious disease during its acute phase. It is critical to wait at least twenty-four hours after any fever before you restart an exercise plan, and even then begin slowly.

Many doctors are reluctant to suggest exercises in any case where a patient's health has been questionable. If you, in fact, have a doubt about your doctor's recommendation, you may wish to seek out one who is exercise-oriented. He is more likely to have seen people perform these programs safely, and may be better able to evaluate your position.

While health itself can be a limiting factor, age never is.

You are literally never too old to get in shape. In San Francisco, a man named Larry Lewis at the age of a hundred and six ran the 100-yard dash in seventeen seconds. A hotel waiter, Lewis had been a regular jogger since the age of eighty. He jogged six miles every morning in Golden Gate Park, then walked five miles to work, where he put in eight hours on his feet, and often walked the five miles home.

Of course, once you start—and this applies as much to you and me as to Larry Lewis—you must continue your program. One medical study has shown that young men between twenty and twenty-five, who trained vigorously up to an hour, five or six times a week, for up to six months and then stopped still showed some minor continued "training effect" up to as much as six months later. But men forty to forty-five, after three months of similar conditioning, lost all of their benefits within six weeks. So the older we get the faster we lose it, and the more careful we must be to maintain ourselves.

After you have selected your exercise, seen the doctor, taken the stress test and had a program prescribed, you need to think about the right equipment. Such as:

Walking or Jogging. You will need a quality shoe. *Runner's World* magazine rates as the top five: New Balance, Nikey Waffle Trainers, Brooks Villanova, Etonic and Adidas TRX. Of course, the ideal way to walk or jog is with bare feet on thick grass. Also, it is wise to dress in comfortable, casual, light clothes.

Swimming. Pick a suit that is unconfining, unless, of course, you live in a rather liberal neighborhood and plan to go *au naturel.* It helps to swim in a pool, or body of water, large enough so that you will not get bored by making three hundred repetitions to get one mile of exercise.

Cycling. A ten-speed bike is preferable but not imperative. It is critical to have the seat adjusted properly. The weight of the body should be distributed in three areas: (1) on the shoulders, leaning forward on the handlebars; (2) on the hips, which rest on the seat, and (3) on the legs, working the pedals. For the indoor athlete, the stationary bike, called an ergometer, is effective. Models sell for between $80 and $250—tax deductible if prescribed by your doctor.

Cross-Country Skiing. Obviously, you will need warm clothes, good skis, poles and shoes, powdery snow and a cozy cabin. It is important to use good sense, follow safety precautions and make sure you have proper maps.

Golf. If you ride a cart you might as well spend the time watching television, for all the good you are doing your heart. Golf is not an aerobic sport even if you walk, but it beats riding. According to Ken Cooper, it takes 180 holes of golf to equal one and a half hours of jogging.

Tennis. You need a racquet that feels right, comfortable togs and good shoes. Tennis is more beneficial than golf. Any time you engage in an exercise in which your heart rate goes up and down—no matter how briefly it goes down —you are erasing part of the cardiovascular effects. In tennis you get a fast volley going and your heartbeat goes up very high, to 180 or 190, and then there is a lull and it drops. That is why tennis players don't do nearly as well on the treadmill as joggers.

This doesn't mean you should throw away your racquet or your golf clubs. By all means, keep them for the fun factor, but supplement them with one of the more effective aerobic exercises.

Once you begin a program, it is important to know that your heart and lungs will not be the things that limit you. They can take it. Your progress is more likely to be interrupted by the shin splint, the ankle pain, or that Achilles pull. If you walk, jog or run on a regular basis your legs will condition themselves. But where you will need help, and will need to exercise care, is *before* you give the order "Feets, do your stuff."

This is where your five-minute warm-up period comes in, no matter what your program may be—squash, handball, jogging, swimming, cycling, tennis, or you name it. No activity should be attempted while your body is still tight and rigid. So these exercises are designed to prevent 95 percent of all exercise-related injuries. They will build your leg muscles, stimulate your circulation and get you loose.

Toe Touches. Keeping the knees locked, bend forward and touch the toes, or go as far down as you can. Do not jerk or bounce in the stretched position. Repeat this *six* times. Now unlock the knees and bend over again, this time concentrating on a maximum stretch for the lower-back muscles. Repeat this *six* times. This movement stretches the long muscles on the back of the thighs and activates the lower back.

Step-Outs. Stand with your feet nearly together, almost at military attention. Step out one long stride, keeping the rear foot firmly planted. Hold for thirty seconds. Allow the forward knee to bend, then stretch and return. Repeat with the opposite leg. This exercise affects the groin area particularly, as well as most of the muscles of the legs.

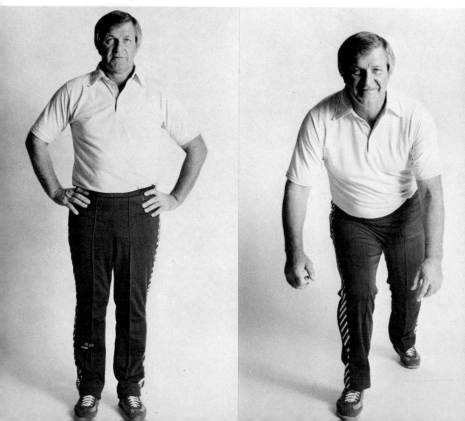

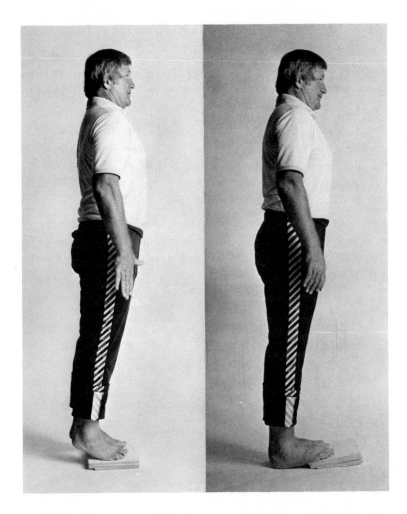

Achilles Stretch. With the toes and balls of the feet elevated on a block of wood or a curb or even a thick book, let the heels descend, stretching the calf muscles and the Achilles tendons. Raise up onto your toes and the balls of your feet. Hold for thirty seconds and repeat. This movement keeps the Achilles tendon flexible, as well as the muscles of the calf.

The Half Knee Bend. As you get older, the full knee bend can turn into a real knee popper. But the half measure will still give your thigh and calf muscles plenty of work. Stand with your feet about eight inches apart and place a two- or three-inch book under your heels. Hold your arms straight in front of you at shoulder level for balance. Keep your upper body erect as you lower your hips to the

seat level of an ordinary dining room chair. You may actually place a chair behind you, so that your rump touches the edge of it each time to remind you that you have gone far enough. Return to an upright position. Repeat *six* times. Concentrate on using the muscles in your calves as you straighten your legs. The concentration should be focused on the calf because your thigh muscles will naturally get enough of the work.

These four movements will flex and stretch the most critical areas involved in running or jogging. They will help keep your muscles supple and give them a protection from stress-related injuries. These are *not* calisthenics and should be performed in a slow, deliberate manner.

When you are warming up, don't neglect the shoulders, especially if your game is tennis or handball or any of the sister sports. But even in jogging the shoulders tend to get tight. So it is a good idea to include a series of jumping jacks or windmills. They are not tiring or difficult, and twenty should be a reasonable number.

The jumping jack is the one that often starts the day on many military bases; and you will recognize it from pregame football drills. You slap your hands over your head while kicking the legs apart, and slap your sides as the legs come together.

In windmills you simply swing your arms around in a circular fashion, extended from your side.

For the beginner, the guiding principle should be "Train, don't strain." Begin your exercise—be it walking, jogging, swimming or cycling—slowly, and build up over a period of two or three minutes. You can check yourself by the simplest of devices, the "talk test." Never jog so fast that

you cannot talk to a partner who is exercising with you. If you can manage only one word per breath, slow down.

If nothing else works, you can be reassured by the fact that you have a "saver." If you don't own a bicycle and don't want one, if you don't live near water, if you haven't the will to run or the room to jog, you can always walk. Even if you are a truly lazy lump who cannot bring himself to follow anything that is regimented, you have the advantage of already knowing how to walk.

In a survey of four thousand doctors, walking was rated the easiest and safest way to fight shortness of breath, overweight, an ailing heart and all the other ills that go with advancing age and too much flab.

Walking is the one activity you can perform in the course of your everyday routine and count on your better-health scorecard. It also qualifies as a preconditioner. That is, many doctors suggest up to three weeks of brisk walking before you attempt any kind of running program.

For a sample program, you can break it down in this way, using a five-day schedule:

First week: Walk a mile a day.

Second week: Walk a mile and a half a day.

Third week: Walk for 100 counts, run for 100 counts, while doing your mile and a half.

Fourth week: Run a mile, walk a half.

Fifth week: You are ready to run.

For centuries people walked because they had no choice, or it was a pleasant way to pass time in the company of someone they liked. But as a health builder, walking re-received a boost in the early 1950s when Dr. Paul Dudley

White recommended it for his most famous patient, Dwight Eisenhower, during the President's recovery from a heart attack.

Ike chose to do his walking on the golf course, and we know now that golf is among the less effective recreations. Keep in mind that the average American male takes in more than 3,000 calories a day, but he requires only about 2,600. Those extra 400 calories are what cause most of our problems. The average golfer burns up only 250 calories in an hour on the links, and two martinis in the clubhouse afterward will put those back, if not more.

As we have noted, golfers stop and go with too much lag time between trips. Just a plain old-fashioned walk, at a fairly brisk and even pace, will give virtually every part of the human body a workout while reducing to a minimum the factors of strain and fatigue. Yet walking is probably our most neglected exercise. Time is the main obstacle. We are all in too much of a hurry, even when we have nothing else to do. So the trick is to work five miles or so of walking into your weekly routine.

Here are three suggestions that will make it easy on you:

1. Pick a parking lot six to eight blocks from your office. The length of the block depends on where you live, but I'm talking about a half mile. The round trip will add a mile a day to your work week, but it could be a valuable mile. You will have to get up a bit earlier and to bed a bit earlier, and that is a healthy combination in itself. You can use the morning walk to plan the first few hours of your day. The evening walk can give you time to unwind.

2. If you live a long stroll from a news vendor, don't sub-

scribe to the Sunday paper. Hike for it instead. Who knows?
Your walk might even take you near a church.

3. Get in the habit of walking to the store for the things
you (or your roommate) forgot to buy.

For your reference only, I'm going to lay out additional
samples of four aerobic exercise programs, designed for a
forty-year-old executive with a normal electrocardiogram
but a low fitness rating. Again, a caution: you should *not*
undertake or adapt these programs to your own use without first consulting your family doctor. The idea is not to
turn you loose, but to give you an understanding of how a
well-rounded routine works.

It is strongly recommended that you follow the program
every other day. This schedule builds in a layoff that ac-
complishes two goals: it allows the ligaments to rest, and
it lightens the mental load. You will be averaging three
to four workouts a week, which will get the job done without burning up your motor.

JOGGING

Week	Activity	Distance (miles)	Time Goal (minutes)
1	Walk	1.0	18:00
2	Walk	1.5	23:00
3	Walk/Jog	1.0	13:00
4	Walk/Jog	1.0	11:00
5	Walk/Jog	1.5	17:00
6	Jog	1.5	15:00
7	Jog	1.5	14:00
8	Jog	2.0	20:00
9	Jog	2.0	19:00
10	Jog	2.0	18:00

CYCLING

Week	Distance	Time
1	4.0	16:30
2	5.0	21:30
3	3.0	13:00
4	4.0	15:30
5	5.0	19:45
6	3.0	11:30
7	5.0	19:00
8	6.0	23:15
9	6.0	23:00
10	8.0	31:30

STATIONARY CYCLING

Week	Distance	Speed (mph)
1	5.0	15
2	5.0	20
3	5.0	15
4	7.5	20
5	10.0	15
6	10.0	20
7	11.0	15
8	11.0	20
9	12.0	15
10	12.0	20

TREADMILL

Week	Speed (mph)	Time
1–2	2.5–3.0	15:00
3–4	3.0	18:00
5–6	3.0–3.5	12:00
7–8	3.0–3.5	15:00

Week	Speed (mph)	Time
9–10	3.0–3.5	18:00
11–12	3.5–4.0	12:00
13–14	3.5–4.0	14:00
15–16	3.5–4.0	16:00
17–18	4.0	12:00
21	4.0	15:00
22	4.0	14:00
23	4.0	13:00

And now a few final tips from an old pro:

1. One of the more critical times is immediately after vigorous exercises, when you should employ a five- to ten-minute cool-down period by performing a slow activity, such as walking. Never stop suddenly and sit down immediately after exercise. (I love race horses and go to the track often. You never see a horse stopped short after a hard run.) Be certain that you cool down for at least ten minutes prior to showering.

2. Should you find that you are unable to advance from one week to another in your program, you should go back and repeat the first week again, and do this each time until you find that you can achieve the next stage. The last level of exercise in each program is the minimum considered necessary to attain the training effect you want, and to qualify you for the good-to-excellent category of fitness.

3. Do not eat directly before exercising. Generally, solids should be avoided two hours before running, especially in hot weather. It is important, however, to drink plenty of fluids. Ten ounces or more of any one of the "ade" drinks should be taken within ten minutes of any running activity when the day is hot, and every twenty to thirty minutes

thereafter. These fluids contain a high concentration of sugar and can be taken as long as they are well diluted. If they are not properly diluted they can cause an accumulation of fluid in the stomach and bring on diarrhea. In the 1976 Boston Marathon, in which the temperatures were extremely high, many runners did indeed suffer from diarrhea as they attempted to finish the race. Needless to say, such a condition adds an element of excitement that an athlete can do without.

4. An important decision is when to do your running (or exercising). Medically, there is no ideal time to run. Some prefer the end of the day. Executives often consider this the best time because it helps to get rid of the tensions that accumulate at the office. But the most popular time, if you surveyed people, would be in the morning, between six-thirty and seven. People who stick with their program the most are morning exercisers (only a 30 percent dropout rate, as opposed to 60 percent for the night hawks.) The main thing is to fit the workout into your life style. Dr. George Sheehan, the author of several books on physical fitness, jogs during his lunch hour; he is too sleepy in the morning and too tired at night. Washington's most prominent jogger, Senator William Proxmire, jogs on his way to work. "If I go by car during the rush hour," he says, "it would probably take me twenty-five minutes. I run that five miles in thirty-five minutes. So the difference is only ten minutes and I get a tough, aerobic workout."

5. Be alert for symptoms of overexertion: chest pain, dizziness, lightheadedness and nausea. It is important to check your recovery heart rate. This can be done five minutes after you have completed the exercise by checking your pulse—counting the number of beats in ten seconds

and multiplying by six. If your heart rate remains at about 120, then you have been exercising too vigorously.

6. Adjust to changes in temperature. A stroll on a hot day doubles the body's heat production. A sprint briefly increases it a hundredfold. A nice day for tanning beside the pool may be a disastrous one for running. As the inside heat goes up, the body compensates by sweating. These lost fluids have to be replaced by water and other chemicals. If more than 3 to 5 percent of the body weight is lost by sweating, your performance is affected. If much more is lost, health itself is threatened. If you must run in hot weather, weigh yourself before and after. Don't be afraid to drink while you exercise, and replace the liquids you are losing. The old theory about avoiding water when you're hot has long been outdated. Remember, sweat cools you as it evaporates. If the humidity is high, sweat does not evaporate as well. Use not only the temperature as your guide, but the level of humidity as well. During a game at Miami in 1975, ten San Francisco players suffered heat prostration, and several had to be given intravenous fluids on the plane returning home.

7. When the weather is cold, you don't get any points for pretending you belong to the Polar Bear Club. The body can adjust to cold as long as you cover up. So break out the long johns and a good pair of gloves. There is no danger to the lungs from inhaling icy air, but keep in mind that the wind tends to add to the chill factor. Every mile of wind drops the chill reading by about one degree, so a twenty-degree temperature with a twenty-mile-an-hour wind is equal to roughly zero weather. I have always been championship-oriented, but I'm glad I missed the famous Dallas–Green Bay "ice bowl" in 1967, when the wind chill

factor reduced the temperatures to forty below. The referees' whistles actually froze to their lips. (Some players may have seen this as a plus.) All weather conditions are tolerable *if* you dress and act appropriately.

You may have noticed by now that this is the longest chapter in the book, essentially because it *is* the guts of the book. For most of us who are over forty we are at a station in life that might be described as third-and-twenty. What I'm trying to tell you is where your next play is coming from.

CHAPTER V

The Repair Department

Probably the first thing that is going to happen to you when you start a regular exercise program of *any* kind is that you'll experience some form of physical distress. I mean you'll start hurting.

This isn't exactly preventable, though a lot of it can be avoided by a proper warm-up. Most of the trouble stems from the fact that you can't apply the axle grease until you know what axle is squeaking. Then you can deal with it.

Sometimes, especially in professional sports, the injury syndrome is something that requires a Sherlock Holmes. I have observed many interesting cases of injury unraveling.

There was a three-year period at Oakland when we had thirty-seven injuries to the quadraceps (front of thigh) and hamstrings (back of thigh). Dr. Reedy added them up and was astounded to find that thirty-five of the injuries were to offensive players. That's a clue, right?

Dr. Reedy began checking around, but he didn't limit himself to quizzing the other NFL doctors and trainers. He talked with people in the pro basketball league, and then with major-league baseball trainers. It turned out that basketball players rarely had any of these injuries, and neither did most of the baseball players—except occasionally the outfielders. Another clue!

Ah, it was elementary, my dear Watson. The guys who ran backwards—such as basketball players on defense, or defensive men on pass coverage, or infielders retreating for a fielding play—had fewer of these troubles. The guys who ran forward, including outfielders who turned and chased a fly ball, were the ones susceptible.

Dr. Reedy then prescribed a program of stretching exercises and backward running for all our offensive players, especially the ones who had had an injury of this kind. We immediately showed a significant drop in thigh injuries.

If you think this has little to do with the problems you find at the outset of your own exercise program, you are wrong. Here are the most common problems, and a way to correct them or at least cope:

The Achilles Tendon. This is the tendon or heel cord just above the back of the ankle, extending to the heel. If you're a dedicated sports fan, you will be aware that a lot of careers have been ended when an Achilles tendon tears apart. (The name comes from the Greek myth in which Achilles was supposed to be rendered immune to injury when he was submerged in the River Styx. But when Achilles was dipped into the magical river by his mother she held on to his heel, and so it didn't get wet. He was eventually brought down by an injury to this portion of his body. From that legend we get both the phrase "Achilles heel," meaning a vulnerable spot, and the medical term "Achilles tendon.")

I have known pro football athletes who learned by hard experience that Achilles-tendon trouble would limit their playing time. One of them walked around all the off season at his home in a special pair of clogs that raised his toes four inches higher than his heels. The following season he played fourteen games and caught over a thousand yards' worth of passes.

Here's how to combat your own Achilles problem: Stand barefoot, with your feet together, facing a wall. Place the toes against the wall and bend at the knees. The knees should touch the wall without the heels being raised from the floor. If you can accomplish the same test with the toes three inches from the wall, you have adequate flexibility. If you can touch it at four inches, you can forget about Achilles trouble.

Knees and Thighs. Stand on a step with feet together and knees locked in a straight position with the toes even with the front edge. Bend forward at the waist and reach downward toward the toes. Hold for thirty seconds. You should be able to touch the top of your arch without strain. If you can touch your toes at the level of the step, your knee flexibility is adequate. The ability to reach beyond the step level at least four inches indicates you'll have little if any hamstring (back of thigh) trouble.

Hips. Lie on your back on a bench or table with your hips near the end. Grasp the right knee with both hands

and pull it slowly toward your chest, allowing the opposite leg to relax or hang over the edge of the table. Bring the right knee as close as possible to the shoulder. This tests the left hip flexors for flexibility. If your left leg comes up above the horizontal you have considerable tightness in the area. If the left leg remains horizontal during the pulling of the right knee, you have reasonable flexibility. If the left leg remains hanging below the table level, you can be assured of having good flexibility in the front of the hip region. Repeat the test with the opposite hip by bringing the left knee toward the shoulder, etc.

The Lower Back. This is one of the greatest areas of poor muscle control that any doctor sees in his practice. A lot of people have poor flexibility and poor muscle tone, especially in the abdominal region. This is undoubtedly one of the most critical areas of muscle flexibility that needs to be dealt with.

Dr. Reedy has seen some 80 to 90 percent of all low-back problems referred to him after long-term difficulty respond thoroughly, with no medicines, after six to eight weeks of vigorous twice-a-day exercises. He has prescribed exercises for the low back and the neck that require only four minutes of activity, and this routine has helped immensely.

This is the way to define your back troubles—that is, the degree of tightness in those muscles:

First step: Kneel on the floor, sitting on your heels. Bend your trunk forward as far as possible, resting the buttocks on your heels. You should have no trouble laying your head on the ground in front of your knees unless your back is extremely tight.

Second step: Sit on the floor with legs straight and feet

about three feet apart. Now bend the head and shoulders toward the right knee. Then to the left. If you can touch your forehead to each knee, your back and hamstring (back of thigh) flexibility can be considered good.

Third step: Assume a sitting position on the floor, your legs straight in front and feet together. Place an eight-inch book edgewise between the knees and bend the head forward until the forehead touches the book. If you succeed, you have the greatest low-back hamstring flexibility.

Note: In all of the above three steps, if you should fail to meet the requirements, go as far as you can comfortably, then repeat at regular intervals until you achieve these specified goals.

Those are the elemental exercises to control the various problems that a regular exercise program may incur. But by far the greatest trouble is in the lower back, and many a fellow has given up on exercise simply because his back has hurt him so much—even walking, let alone jogging or any other kind of strenuous exercise.

I have been around a lot of guys who had back trouble, and these were people whose very professional existence depended on their beating the problem. An office guy can complain of back pains. But if you're making $90,000 a year in the NFL and your back begins to plague you, *that's* pressure.

Supposedly, the one thing that can correct a back problem is the sit-up exercise. But there are sit-ups and sit-ups. The old-timey way had a guy sit on a chair with his legs outstretched, his feet hooked under a rung, his hands clasped behind his neck, and then he would lurch himself upward to touch his right elbow against his left knee. This one regimen did more to *cause* back trouble than anything else ever devised by man. The stark effort required to raise the torso against that kind of pressure was immense, and counterproductive.

The truth is, of course, that abdominal (stomach) strength is the greatest way to relieve lower-back pain and strain. But you have to be cautious in the remedy. As follows:

Lie on your back on the floor with your knees bent and feet flat. Raise the arms and reach toward the knees, raise the chin to the chest, and the shoulders and upper back off the ground, as you reach toward the knees with the hands. Hold a "partial sit-up" position for twenty seconds.

Repeat this partial sit-up ten to twenty times, with rest in between. When you are able to repeat this for approximately twenty seconds up to fifty times, you will have reached the necessary abdominal-muscle strength.

Tightening of the abdominal muscles is the most significant solution for low-back strain and the pain that comes with it.

Knee and Hip Exercise. The strength of the knee and hip muscles can be measured by machine, but a simpler way is by doing the partial-squat knee bend. The knee bend, done with your hands clasped atop head, should be stopped when the thigh is parallel to the floor. This means that the buttocks should be level with the knee, never lower. (The full deep knee bend which used to be part of military and football drills is a dangerous exercise that frequently resulted in *knee injury*, especially among older people.)

The knee bend should be accomplished twenty-five times for good muscle power and conditioning. Then the desired leg strength can be determined by the number of single leg bends you can do (holding on to something for stability).

When you can complete ten bends on each leg, you're at your goal.

These are the common causes of knee problems:

1. Cheap or wrong-size running shoes which fail to give proper support (as I noted in the previous chapter).

2. Running on a slanted surface, as on the side of a pitched roadway. This will cause a strain in the back of the high-ground knee. One solution is an equal-distance run on the opposite side of the road. But it's better to avoid sloping runways altogether.

3. Running downhill. Even experienced long-distance runners have suffered hip and groin and back pain in this way. The solution: Run uphill, walk downhill.

4. The most common cause: The problems begin in the feet, and as the leg tries to compensate, the knee suffers.

Foot and Toe Muscles. The most common problem of the foot is called "Morton's toe." (The pain wasn't named in honor of quarterback Craig Morton; it was named for the doctor who first diagnosed the trouble.) This results from an abnormally shortened first toe, in which the little bones under the joint become overly movable and show some arthritis. You know you've got it when you suffer a burning pain between the first and second toes.

The solution is a small pad or an arch support to get the pressure off the front of the foot and distribute the weight equally. It may be necessary to have an orthopedist construct a small plastic support that will properly balance the foot. This is called an "orthotic."

A second major problem in the foot is a sharp pain leading from the heel to the long arch of the foot. Dr. Reedy tells me this is called Plantar Fasciitis. Arch supports can be very effective here too. Anti-inflammatory medicines or aspirin should be taken two to four times a day for one week. If it doesn't go away, that means another trip to the foot doctor.

Next is a heel spur, the kind of injury that sidelined Joe Di Maggio long ago and Arthur Ashe more recently. For our purposes it can be cared for quite easily with a heel pad constructed like a doughnut, placing the hole in the pad directly underneath where the pain is. This pad must be thick enough to get pressure off the heel, but not so thick that it lifts the heel out of the shoe. It is also important to put a pad of equal thickness under the heel of the other foot. If you don't, you will be running slightly out of balance and cause more leg or knee problems on the other side.

Shin Splints. No matter the sport, football or basketball or soccer, every athlete at one time or another has suffered with shin splints. There are probably five or six different causes of this pain. It's defined as pain in the front of the leg, usually on the inside edge of the shinbone extending about midway from the calf down toward the ankle.

Very often it's related to poor stretching during warm-up exercises, poor heel cushions on shoes, or a variety of foot problems. In mild form, shin splints will disappear with proper warmup time, after a couple of days of rest, and avoidance of uphill courses. If it persists, the best remedy is the use of natural vitamin E, 1,600 units each day. This is defined as d-alpha tocopherol. It increases the blood supply to the legs and feet. Within ten days to two weeks, the pain should be erased.

Some people have to continue taking this organic and

natural vitamin E for as long as they exercise. This is an over-the-counter item.

Chronic Neck Pain. This is something that gave me a lot of trouble for several weeks not long ago. Anyone can get a sort of arthritic stiff neck, but I was told that mine probably came from some mild knock I took along the way, or some jerking mechanism during a workout or even around the house. In any case, the problem gets worse when you try to keep your neck in a position that won't feel pain, or even try to turn your neck to look to one side or the other. Then it is constant discomfort for the neck to do its job.

Here's how to build up those muscles again and end the problem:

1. Standing erect and keeping the shoulders straight, bend your left arm back of your head and place the palm of your left hand on the rear upper right side of your head, above and slightly back of your ear.

2. Cock your right hand back at the wrist as far as it will go and place its heel against the under left side of your jaw.

3. Using both in a gentle but firm pressure, twist your head to the right as far as it will go comfortably. Then go a little farther—past comfort but not to pain. Hold for ten seconds and release.

4. Do six to eight repetitions and then reverse the entire procedure, this time twisting the head to the left.

The exercise is guaranteed to do wonders for older men who have difficulty craning their necks at a pretty girl walking down the beach.

There are some basic things about injuries:

Faulty equipment. With runners, this usually means shoes which are either inadequate or worn out. With cyclists, it is almost always the improper setting of the seat. It should be at a level so that weight is equally distributed to your shoulders as they are supported by your hands on the handlebar, your hips by the seat and your legs by a proper extension. The rule for seat height: When the pedal is at the bottom of the cycle the knee should be bent about five degrees.

Overwork. You have tried to do too much too soon in too short a period of time, and your body is rebelling. Slow down, relax, give the muscles time to become more flexible and less rigid, and give yourself more time to get to the level of capacity you would like to be. Remember, you spent most of your life getting your body into the shape it's in now, so don't try to correct matters overnight.

Weakness and inflexibility. These flaws can be remedied one by one, as your exercise program continues.

Mechanical problems. These are faults in the running form, such as the way the foot hits the ground.

Injury protection can be accomplished entirely by using good sense with the flexibility warmup, taking time to get adequate warmup before starting to exercise, taking an adequate cool-down period and, finally, flexibility exercises after the workout.

The magazine *Runner's World* conducted a poll of its readers not long ago and found that two thirds of the runners had suffered an injury serious enough to stop their training during the first year of workouts, and, secondly, that most of them had been hurt more than once.

So something bad will probably happen to anyone during a program of regular exercise. The solution is not to let this discourage you from continuing. There is usually a simple way to cope with any problem.

CHAPTER VI

What Did I Do Right?

The first rule of getting it together is not to feel sorry for yourself. Whatever habits or weaknesses have held you back, you are not alone. If you were one of a kind, chances are you would have been stuffed long ago and shipped to the Smithsonian.

In fact, your case probably isn't much different from my own. I was a fat kid. Lazy most of my life. A three-packs-a-day smoker. But an expert, after all, is someone who has already made his mistakes.

First, let's take up the business of cigarettes. There are no more devout missionaries than reformed smokers, as we all know. They will lecture total strangers in elevators, on airplanes, in a church or jail. That isn't my style. But I will tell you what I did wrong, why I stopped and how, and you can draw your own conclusions.

I was your classic procrastinator. I always told myself I

77

could give up smoking whenever I wanted. In point of fact, I did, while I was with the Houston Oilers in 1963. I didn't smoke again until 1967, when I signed with Oakland. I'd smoke a cigar now and then, and the other players complained about them. There are always card games going on in the locker room and on the team plane. You always have time to kill, and you sit around getting nervous or bored and you want something in your hand. I reached a point where I would take a drag off someone else's cigarette, and the next thing I knew I was smoking two or three packs again.

I didn't inhale, or so I thought. The truth is that you do so even inadvertently, and enough smoke gets into your system to have an effect. But I justified the habit by saying to myself, "Well, I don't inhale and blow it out my nose and that kind of garbage, so I'm not hurting myself."

But I would get up in the morning coughing heavily. I finally connected that with smoking, and one day I just said, "I quit." I made up my mind that I didn't want to wake up coughing anymore. That was the day of my last cigarette, the first week in April 1975.

I like to think that I am a very positive person. If something interferes with how I feel, then I have to get rid of it. I'm a light drinker for the same reason. I always felt that liquor affected my conditioning.

Of course, everyone who needs to quit smoking has to be aware of one usual side effect. My weight went up when I stopped, and I had to struggle to bring it down. You have to be a disciplined person to give up smoking and develop the right eating habits. I won't soft-soap you, it can be difficult. Which is why so many ex-smokers walk around feeling and acting so righteous.

Of course, the metabolism of certain people will allow them to eat anything, do anything, with no problem. But a lean body and good conditioning do not necessarily go hand in hand. If you just have a thin frame with no muscle, you might as well be a hat rack.

In my conversations with Dr. Reedy, he listed eight areas of my life style and exercise planning, things I do instinctively, that are medically sound and correct in human terms. I have always tried to be aware of ways to help my cardiovascular system. When you hit the Big Four-Oh, the heart is the whole ball game. Why not draw up your own checklist:

1. Be consistent. Everyone responds better to a fixed routine. Exercise has been an ongoing part of my daily world since I was a schoolchild; not for a season or a few months, but year round. Maintaining a program is even more essential, now that I no longer have football to push me or to provide an outlet for the calories I store. So even when I'm on the banquet trail, I make it a point to follow a routine, twenty-five or thirty minutes a day of getting in whatever I need, jogging or handball or cycling.

2. Have fun. I chose the sports I felt I would enjoy most. Exercise doesn't *have* to be a fellowship of pain. Fortunately, I enjoy most games—golf, racquet ball, bowling, ping pong, whatever. Obviously the ones that work your heart and lungs for more extended periods will be the most beneficial. But there is no rule that says you can't have fun whatever you do, even if it is pitching pennies against a crack. The best way to accomplish this is not to exercise alone. Draft a friend. Organize a group. Include your family. Invite someone you need to know better.

3. Stick with it. Whatever I do, I stay with it long

enough to feel the effects. I have never been a faddist. Some people try whatever comes along, almost week to week. A fellow appears selling Transcendental Meditation, they try TM. Then they hear about health foods, and the next time you see them they are living on honey and seeds. After that it might be yoga or quoits. I'm not knocking anything if it helps. I'm only saying, sign up for the duration.

4. Adopt an outlook. Physical fitness should be a life style, not a crash course or a treatment. This means not only finding an activity that will be fun or a challenge, but making it consistent with the way you manage your life. Change your pace, your scenery, the rhythm of your work-day. Quit trying to beat all the stop lights. Relax.

5. See the doctor. This was not altogether by choice, but as a professional football player I was required to have annual physical exams and frequent checkups, and I found this to be a habit worth developing. And this is no time to be bashful. I always asked questions: What had the doctor found? What else should I be doing? I made it a point to be a good historian of my own medical past. This helps make the doctor's job easier, and he is not someone you want to leave guessing.

6. Choose good tools. I have never considered myself a reckless spender, but I don't skimp in terms of the equip-ment I use. I buy quality: shoes, gloves, clubs or software. Many injuries are too often the result of poor and shoddy equipment.

7. Be injury-smart. A pro athlete sometimes has a judg-ment to make about injuries: If it seems slight, do you seek attention and run the risk of being benched or, worse, get a label for coddling yourself? In this area I tried to use

common sense, and so should you. I had a sore right elbow my last couple of years with the Raiders. I didn't talk about it. As long as I only had to kick, and the pain was not significant, I handled it myself. If an activity causes a problem, don't do it. Just remember the gag about the doctor who asked a patient if it hurt when he swung his arm like this. "Yes," the patient replied. "Then stop swinging your arm like that." When the elbow began to limit me, I went to Dr. Reedy. He decided I had a form of tennis elbow and suggested that I sleep with my elbow in a support. The pain went away. I had been sleeping with my arm above my shoulder, straining the muscles.

But one should avoid going to a doctor with every minor soreness. That smacks too much of bringing a slip from home to get out of gym class. For the record, I took some rough smashes in my time and I don't think I ever really bitched about them. I was hurt seriously only once, in 1954, when I suffered a shoulder separation that just about finished me as the Bears' Number 1 quarterback. I was "sandwiched" by Don Colo and Len Ford of the Cleveland Browns.

8. Have a goal. It is important to decide what you want out of your exercise. People start a program for three reasons: to condition their heart and lungs, to help them relax, and to tone their bodies. But I believe it helps to set a specific target, a lower resting pulse rate after so many weeks, or a higher oxygen intake, or a set loss of weight. If a fellow weights 220 and wants to get down to 190, he can say, "I know I'll look better and feel better. And I'll probably live longer." Deep breathing, which is what aerobics is all about, delays the aging process. To keep your cardiovascular system in shape you have to exert yourself.

9. Be portable. Traveling certainly can change your program, but it is no excuse for goofing off. It all depends on whether you want a slim, trim body or whether you are content to get fat and sassy. If you have a routine, you should continue it on the road. Ideally, you should still get in your twenty-five to thirty minutes of jogging—at a park or a YMCA or, if necessary, just around the hotel. A half hour of situps, pushups and run-in-place, all done in your hotel room, to keep your muscles toned. Of course, be careful not to overeat or overdrink. Do your normal exercises, at your usual time, and you can maintain a well-conditioned body.

10. Allow for age. As you grow older you should start eating less. Your meals get smaller. Often this will occur instinctively. Your body gives you a signal and you simply adjust to the obvious: the older you get, the less weight you should carry. You don't burn off the calories as fast. The average male gains one pound a year, and loses a half pound of lean body mass, between the ages of thirty and forty-five. As you grow older, it helps to have pride. Mine kept me going after the Bears didn't want me in 1959, and the Oilers let me go in 1967, and the Raiders put me on the cab team in 1970. Without pride I would have never left Youngwood. I'd have worked for the railroad or in the mines or at the Robertshaw Thermostat Company.

11. Stay high on life—I mean avoid pills, reducing schemes and dope. People want exotic answers when the best ones are so simple. The boxer Archie Moore once said he had been given a special weight-reducing formula from an old Maori shepherd in New Zealand. Maybe so, but he must have lost the only copy, because the last time I saw

Archie he was fat. I still eat basically the same food my mother used to put on the table back in Youngwood, except a little lighter on the potatoes. I have never needed, or taken, drugs. A young player who was my teammate briefly on the Raiders, Chip Oliver, once claimed in a book he wrote that he kicked a seventy-five-yard field goal while he was high on mescaline. Well, I once punted a ball eighty-six yards at Kentucky, and at the time I was high on nothing but Polish sausage.

Another rebel of that time frame, Dave Meggysey—*militants,* they were called in the late 1960s—once asked me if I didn't find it galling, having to go through bedchecks at age forty-three? I told him, "No, I don't find it galling at all. It's one of the rules. If you want to do something, such as play football, you have to abide by the rules." I believe in rules and discipline and a lot of other ideas that may sound old-fashioned. But for me they work. I don't mind admitting that I also have a little salesmanship and gamesmanship in my inventory. A quarterback has to be that way in order to survive and be successful. I'm an optimist too. I wake up every day believing that good things are going to happen. When I'm wrong, I try to look on the bright side. I agree with the guy who said that halitosis is better than no breath at all.

12. Make it a family affair. Exercise is asexual, and I certainly don't mean to exclude half the population from these pointers. But, speaking as a man, it helps to have a wife who challenges you. Betty is bright and intellectual. She paints and reads heavy books. She majored in dance at college and taught classes in it. And she exercises as faithfully as I do. Once the weather gets warm enough in Chi-

cago, we share a nightly thirty-five- to forty-minute bicycle ride after dinner. We cover five to eight miles, under no pressure, at no set distance or speed.

A family effort should be a vital part of every person's continuing exercise program. In fact, a study that was done among joggers showed that 80 percent of those who had the support of their wives and families kept it up. But of those who did not have family support, only 40 percent continued to exercise. At the least, your wives and kids can help by not hassling you when your workouts take you away from the house. But their help would be much more valuable if they joined in.

Betty has always tried to keep up with me, or even ahead of me. When we were first married she asked my mother for her recipe for kolachies, a kind of Polish cookie. The one my mother used called for *eleven* cups of flour. The first time Betty tried the recipe she had dough strung all over the apartment—the couch, chairs, windowsills, everywhere. She had forgotten that Mama cooked for seven Blanda boys.

There is one other fringe benefit to be derived from involving your family. A bicycle ride, a jog, a long walk, can be a mighty fine way to give attention to the quiet problems of your children, individually, at a time when you are both relaxed and unhurried.

CHAPTER VII

Packing in the Groceries

I am supposed to be a fine one to talk about food, because I was for so many years a professional football player. But, believe me, the demands for food go by position.

After a game, I have seen one of our offensive linemen, a 260-pound specimen, put down a quart of orange juice, a large bowl of minestrone and a complete Dover sole dinner. This was his appetizer. Then he stowed away a baked potato and Chateaubriand steak for two, followed by a whole cherry pie and another quart of orange juice. A man needs his liquids.

You cannot believe the amount of groceries put away by a pro football team at training camp every summer. I think somebody averaged it out that the players were expending something like 4,300 calories of energy in the two-a-day drills, so if they stowed away 3,500 calories at the chow hall they were still ahead of the game.

I had a different problem. My first pro team was the Chicago Bears, and their blessed owner-coach, George Halas, had an easy formula to derive what his players should weigh: They should weigh, forever, what they weighed when they were seniors in college. But it so happened that when I got out of Kentucky, I was still a growing young man. This fact didn't make a damn bit of difference to Halas. Therefore I went to the Fat Man's Table at training camp. No salt, no starches, all boiled foods.

You worked out under a hot sun for four hours and you couldn't maintain enough strength to pick up a fork. There was a stigma to being at the Fat Man's Table. I used to be there weighing 203 pounds. Ed Sprinkle, the defensive end, was the captain of the Fat Man's Table at 215. We were both thin. But there were guys who were 265 who were not —probably because their college publicist exaggerated their weight in the school program.

What Halas didn't know was that we would weaken ourselves for the weekly Wednesday morning weigh-in and then gorge ourselves on Thursday and Friday and be ten pounds heavier for the game on Sunday. Or maybe Halas planned it that way. I don't know.

What all this means is that I had to make it my business to know what I was eating. Along the way I devised some ways to eat what I wanted without paying the full price for it. I'll share them with you.

The problem is, it is not only *what* you eat, but *how* and *when*. Here are my ten rules for losing weight *without* dieting:

1. Don't skimp breakfast. Here's your best opportunity to store up a lot of nourishment without adding any fat to your goodly supply, so don't pass it up. After a good

night's rest your body is ready to wear off the effects at full speed.

2. Load up at midday. Your noon meal should be the big meal of your day, which is a neat trick, I'll agree, for the working man. If you can afford the added expenditure of time or money or both, don't hesitate. Go home for lunch, if possible. Or find a restaurant that serves something besides sandwiches. You have a hard-working afternoon ahead of you to burn up the groceries.

3. The three-hour fast. If Ghandi could do it for weeks, you can make it the last three hours before bedtime. Avoid TV programs which have food commercials. Put a time lock on your refrigerator. Anything. But eat supper at least three hours before you hit the sack, and nothing afterward, until breakfast.

4. Don't skip a meal. Aside from the wear and tear on your nervous system, skipping a meal (lunch, for instance) may actually cause you to gain weight. The explanation of this has to do with your metabolism. Meanwhile, believe me, the sacrifice of one of your three squares costs you more than it's worth.

5. Don't eat junk between meals. There are two reasons, only one of which is obvious: the added calories. The second is equally important. Between-meal snacks cut down your enjoyment and the fulfillment of the food you will eat at the regular hour. However, munching on fruit or dry roasted nuts is a healthful way to satisfy the "hungries."

6. Don't deny your sweet tooth, just retrain it. Natural sugar—fresh fruit—is the answer. Many nutritionists now recommend that white, refined and even raw sugars be eliminated from the athlete's diet. Nor is honey any longer considered a safe sugar substitute. Parry O'Brien, the Olym-

pic shotput champion of a few yeears ago, popularized honey among trackmen as a quick energizer. But we know now that a teaspoon of honey is three times sweeter than a teaspoon of sugar. (And one Hershey bar has the same amount of sugar as three and a half pounds of apples.)

7. Avoid alcohol. Even though comic Joe E. Lewis used to claim that he saw a lot more old drunks around than old doctors, cut drinking down to a minimum if you want to control weight.

8. Don't omit liquids. Drink at least six glasses of water or natural fruit juices a day. Mainly this is a stipulation for good health.

9. Listen to Grandma. Remember how parents in the old days used to say, "Don't bolt your food"? Then there was the period when psychologists believed that if you insisted a kid chew his food better he might get up from the table and go rob a bank. Anyway, Grandma was right. The greatest single secret for losing weight is the careful mastication of your food before it goes down the pipe. The reason is simple. Food is more *filling* when you chew it thoroughly. Half the trouble with overweight people is that they eat so fast they hardly taste what they eat, and they end by eating more than they really want. This has been more or less certified by the popular Weight Watchers program, which advises everyone to lay down the fork for a few seconds after every bite. Grandma was right about another thing too, when she told you not to slump at the table. An erect posture while eating also helps you cut down on the quantity of your meal.

10. The toughest one: Obey the first nine rules.

A biochemist could devote sixteen hours a day to studying your eating habits and come up with an accurate count of your caloric intake.

Fortunately, we do not need a biochemist to add and sub- tract our calories. The problem is simple. It has only been made complex by people who want to impress us with their immense knowledge of the subject. If you are overweight, you are taking on too many calories, more calories than your body is using in its normal daily activities.

Presumably, you will undertake a continuous program of modest exercise, as prescribed previously. You will be surprised how many calories this slight addition in your physical effort will burn away.

The objective now is to find a new list of menus which will be satisfying, filling and realistic—the kind of change with which you'll be able to live for the rest of your life. And of course the main idea is not to cut down on the *amount* of food you eat but the *kind* of food you eat.

But first let's take a look at the main culprits: meat, potatoes, bread and sweets. Those are the four items on the American dinner table which are 90 percent responsible for most people being overweight. You can't omit them en- tirely, but there are several ways to keep them on the menu without wrecking a program of weight control.

Most people are aware of the foods that add on pounds, or they think they are. A few have some idea of the foods recommended by nutritionists, or think they do. Below you find both of these categories listed in full.

Meat. The main culprit is beefsteak. There are more than 2,000 calories in a pound of prime rib. If you must have an occasional steak, trim away all the fat you can see. The least fattening cut of beef is beef round, so try to confine yourself to it.

The best thing to do about beefsteak is to substitute something else for it. Limit yourself to three entrees a week of meat other than beefsteak, dining on fish or fowl on the other days. Veal loin, veal rib, leg of lamb, calf or beef liver, dried beef in a casserole are tasty ways out of the beefsteak reliance.

Pork, including those juicy slices of breakfast bacon and the salt pork seasoning of vegetable dishes, should be avoided if you want to get anywhere with a weight-losing campaign. Instead, you may eat two slices of Canadian smoked bacon with your morning eggs a couple of times a week. It has 70 percent fewer calories.

Potatoes. It's not so much the poor potato that adds the pounds as what the cook does with it. A medium-size spud, two to three inches thick, represents only 85 calories, and a whale of a lot of goodness—until the skin is trimmed away. Sliced and fried in lard or bacon grease, it is damned near a lethal instrument. The one and only way to take your potato is baked, with a patty or two of corn-oil margarine to make it palatable, skin and all.

Bread. The American variety is the world's most overrated food, a triumph of the ad man and the supermarket over your suffering stomach. The spongy, smooth-textured and comparatively tasteless product got that way because it is more easily merchandised when it "stays fresh longer." What it does is stay spongy longer. There's precious little in it in the first place to keep fresh, and in fact this streamlined staff of life contains no ingredients which you can't get in better and purer form in your regular meals.

Rye and whole-wheat breads are far superior to white bread in vitamin and protein content.

Gluten bread is the answer. Gluten is the nitrogenous part of the flour of wheat which remains behind when the starch is removed by kneading the flour in a current of water. The end result is more expensive, but it is so much lower in calories that it is ideal for people who are trying to lose weight.

Alexander Woollcott, the famous critic, raconteur and fat man, once complained, "Why is it everything I like is either illegal, immoral or fattening?"

Well, that seems to be the way it is with the food list. However, there are a surprising number of good foods which you can eat in satisfying amounts without loading the scales unduly. Let take a reading of that category first.

Preferred Foods

BREAKFAST FOODS

calf kidney

Canadian bacon

coffee or tea (sweetened with honey)

corn grits (not hominy)

corn oil margarine (sparingly)

eggs, boiled or poached

eggs, soft-scrambled in corn oil

melba toast

orange juice, fresh

protein bread

DAIRY PRODUCTS

buttermilk

cottage cheese

skim milk

yogurt

FISH
(not fried)

bass
bluefish
bonito
crabmeat
finnan haddie

halibut
lobster
oysters, raw
shrimp, broiled
trout

FOWL
(not fried)

chicken
pheasant

quail
squab

FRUIT

apples
applesauce, unsweetened
apricots, fresh
cantaloupe
figs, fresh
grapefruit
honeydew melon
lemons
oranges

peaches, fresh or canned
   (unsweetened)
pears, fresh or canned
   (unsweetened)
pineapple, fresh or canned
   (unsweetened)
pineapple juice, unsweetened
strawberries, fresh
tangerines
watermelon

Preferred Foods

MEAT

beef, dried
beef kidneys
beef round
calf brains, kidneys, liver
   tongue
Canadian bacon

lamb kidneys
lamb leg
pig's feet, pickled
rabbit
veal loin or rib
venison

VEGETABLES

artichoke	endive
asparagus	lettuce
bean sprouts	okra
beets	onions, boiled
broccoli	potato, baked
Brussels sprouts	peppers, green
cabbage	radishes
carrots	spinach
cauliflower	squash
celery	stringbeans
cucumbers	tomatoes
eggplant	turnips

The preceding list includes almost a hundred preferred foods that can be included in any weight-loss program. Thousands of excellent dishes may be prepared from this list. (A sampling of recipes will be found in Chapter XI.)

But now we have to be warned about the foods that add pounds to your frame almost as you look at them:

Foods to Avoid

BREAKFAST FOODS

bacon	ham
cold cereals	hominy grits
fried eggs	sausage

DAIRY PRODUCTS

butter	ice cream
cheeses (except cottage)	milk, homogenized
cream	

FISH

herring

mackerel

oysters, fried

sardines

FRUIT

apricots, dried

bananas

cranberry sauce

dates, dried

figs, dried

grapes

plums

prunes, dry or cooked

raisins, dry or cooked

MEAT AND FOWL

beefsteak (most cuts)

duck

goose

pork

turkey

VEGETABLES

corn

hominy

kidney beans

lima beans

navy beans

peas

potatoes, fried or boiled

succotash

sweet potatoes

MISCELLANEOUS

alcoholic beverages*

bakery products

candies

catsup

cocoa

jams and jellies

macaroni

marmalade

nuts (except walnuts)

popcorn

pickles

salad dressing (except olive
oil/vinegar)

spaghetti

syrup

*Note: Two martinis equal one pound sirloin steak.

In summary, the rules for good nutrition are clear and simple: Eat as many fresh foods as you can, including fruit and vegetables, with as much poultry, fowl and fish as possible, with red meat only half as often. Get rid of sugars. Eat often, but in small amounts. Be kind to your body by changing, and purifying, its food supply.

CHAPTER VIII

For Vanity's Sake

Nine out of ten men who are "out of shape" are out of shape where it shows the most—around the middle. The middle, in fact, is where middle age starts, beginning in the early twenties when a guy gives up the active life and assumes the responsibilities of a career, a family, and home mortgages.

The decline of his physique can be measured from front to back as his belt buckle keeps pushing farther and farther ahead of him. The older he gets, the heavier his problem. He has less time to devote to sports (or so he has decided) and the outdoor life, and long ago he lost the inclination to do anything about it.

As I have suggested in this book, the ideal goal of exercise—continuous, slow, long-distance exercises—is to revitalize your heart and lungs. Following any of the exercise programs along this line that you have selected, you will get a natural bonus in the reduction of your waistline.

But some men want to achieve more than that with their bodies, for cosmetic reasons, and I don't blame them. It's an understandable vanity at age forty-five to want to get back to the same silhouette you had twenty or twenty-five years before. And it's not really that difficult.

The midsection is the key to your physique. A man who has a trim waistline will usually have firm muscle tone everywhere else. That's why you should concentrate on the following exercises, which are directed at the upper and lower abdomen (above and below the belt line) and the side rolls of fat at the waistline.

When I say "concentrate" I mean it in the fullest sense of the word. Don't let your mind wander while doing any type of muscular exercise. Send messages to the muscles that are working and you'll get a surprising dividend in results. Otherwise, without your realizing it, your body may bring other muscles into play and void the effect of the exercise. What I'm saying is more or less the same principle as biofeedback, where the mind has done some amazing things in healing the body.

You will notice that these exercises require no special equipment, other than a bath towel and a few kitchen chairs. The only other equipment I would suggest is a pair of five- and ten-pound dumbbells, which can be used very well in a set of hand and arm exercises.

These, of course, are anaerobic exercises, which I mentioned earlier in the book. They are not suggested *in place of* but in addition to the exercise program you have already selected.

The Lower Abdomen

Leg Raises. This one hits below the belt, where most of the trouble is. Men who are slightly overweight first notice the added pounds just under their belt buckles—the potbelly, or paunch.

Pick out a soft place to lie down. Nothing good can come from grating your backbone against a hard floor. Do these exercises on a padded carpet or on a quilt folded once lengthwise.

Lying on your back, put your arms at your sides, palms down, and keep your feet together and legs straight. Now raise your feet eighteen to twenty-four inches. Never bring your feet high enough to gain a resting interval at the peak of the raise. Now lower your feet to within three inches of the starting position. Your feet do not come to rest until the end of the exercise.

Begin with five repetitions and increase by one each session the first week. Increase the repetitions gradually without strain. Within five weeks most of us will have built up to twenty-five repetitions, which is sufficient.

Knee-Outs. This variation of the leg raise will complete your attack on the lower abdomen, an area that is far harder to reduce than the upper abdomen. The knee-out will work the same muscles in a different way, and finally give you a natural web of strength below your belt to hold your stomach flat and trim at all times.

From the same starting position as the Leg Raise, lift your feet together eighteen to twenty-four inches and then bring your knees back toward your chest as far as you can. Now straighten your legs, still without letting your feet rest, and keeping them eighteen to twenty-four inches off the ground.

Start with five repetitions, increase one a day the first

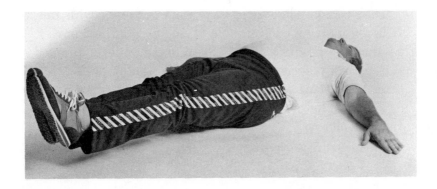

week, then increase gradually so that at the end you will be doing twenty-five repetitions.

Note: Men who are very overweight (twenty pounds or more) can start these two exercises one leg at a time. This is advised for women also. When the one-leg raises and the one-leg knee-outs reach a repetition of twenty-five, start over from the beginning with the two-leg variety.

The Upper Abdomen

Sit-Ups. Now we hit above the belt. This is the most basic of all stomach exercises, and one of the most misunderstood. The U.S. Navy, in its World War II strength test for cadets, awarded points for each repetition up to sixty. Some of those young kids could do 150 or more before moving to the next exercise in the test. Though this might have been good for their characters, the numbers above thirty—without rest intervals—didn't help their physiques at all. High numbers of repetitions *tear down* the very muscles you are trying to build.

The Navy men did the sit-ups with their feet straight and held down by a buddy or anchored under a low rung of gym equipment. They came straight up and alternated touching the right elbow to the left kneecap and the left elbow to the right kneecap.

The average fellow over forty can't get away with this. If he didn't have back trouble to begin with, he'd have it by the time he did a few of these. Even well-conditioned pro football players don't come all the way up on a sit-up. They use a slant board instead to add difficulty and stress.

The ideal for our purposes is the partial sit-up, with hang time, as follows:

Lie down with legs together, knees bent so that your feet are flat on the floor. If possible, have someone hold your ankles, or anchor your feet under a piece of furniture. With hands clasped behind neck, bring the shoulders and the upper back off the floor slowly, and sit up as far as you can. As you reach this point, bring your arms forward and stretch them out in front of you to their limit. Hold this sit-up position for twenty seconds, then return back slowly to original position.

Try to begin with ten repetitions if you can. If not, gradually build up to this number. Over a period of four weeks try to achieve a goal of fifty repetitions, with the twenty-second hang time on each.

The "roll-up" method will avoid strain of the lower-back muscles. As your stomach muscles gain in strength, rely less on the leverage of your arms in bringing you off the floor.

Swedish Reducer. This may sound like something on the menu at a massage parlor, but it is amazingly easy and effective. How would you like to reduce your waistline by two to three inches within thirty days, through one mild exercise alone? The Swedes have devised a way, they say, because they devote so much time and thought to body conditioning. Give it a try. Some find it helpful.

Inhale deeply, then exhale completely. Exhalation is the secret. After all the air has been expelled from your lungs, draw in your stomach until you feel as if it's pressing against your backbone. Hold for a count of five.

That's it. You can perform it several times a day—while shaving, driving to work, at your desk, or in bed in the evening.

Side Bends. The next time you're around someone who claims he doesn't have to do any exercise to stay trim, reach out with your thumb and forefinger and grab the hunk of fat at his side, just above the belt line. Believe me, the fat will be there. Only a concentrated exercise can hit that particular target.

Stand erect with your left palm against your left thigh and your right palm against your right temple. Now bend to the left until your fingertips are just below your left knee. Return to erect position and repeat. Next switch the positions of your hands and bend to the right.

These are the oblique muscles you are conditioning, a final touch if you want a physique that slopes naturally from shoulders to waist.

Begin with five repetitions to each side, increase by one every session for the first week, gradually increase from there to a goal of twenty-five on each side.

Chest, Shoulders, Arms

A businessman's long-sleeved shirt conceals the pounds of flab that hangs on his biceps and pectoral muscles, the inches of suet back of the armpits. A pudgy superstructure does not reveal itself the way a protruding stomach does.

But it is no less a matter of concern for the man who wants to feel younger and look better. Now even the matter of concealment is growing more difficult because of the boom in outdoor living—back-yard swimming pools, cookouts, short-sleeved shirts for office wear.

Unlike the other deposits of fat on the body, these areas are relatively easy to reshape. Your chest, shoulders and arms can be firmed in only a matter of weeks, and the results stick with you, if you keep it up.

There is something about this muscle area that stirs a man's pride in himself as a man. Perhaps it is a throwback to the days when strength was necessary to wrestle a living out of the wilderness. Or perhaps it is the tradition of doting fathers and uncles whose early request of youngsters has always been "Show me your muscles."

The Shoulder Dip. This is an extension of the push-up, and it has a startling way of firming up the pectoral muscles across the top of the chest. The shoulder dip is the most effective way to rid this area of excessive flab. It will also add muscles to widen the shoulders.

Place two straight-back chairs face to face slightly more than shoulder width apart. Place the palms of your hands on the seats of the chairs, not far from the edge. Extend your legs straight behind you, supporting your body on the balls of your feet.

Lower your torso between the two chairs and then push

yourself up to arm's length. Once you have mastered this part of the shoulder dip—ten repetitions without discomfort—move on the the final stage: Place a third chair behind you to elevate your feet. Your body will then be horizontal as if you were doing a push-up at floor level. Lower your torso between the chairs as before and return to arms' length position.

This is a tough exercise, starting out. At the beginning, merely lower yourself to the level of the chair seat. As you gain strength you will be able to dip lower and lower between the chairs, bringing the full results of the exercise.

Over a period of five weeks you should reach a goal of twenty-five repetitions.

The Reverse Dip. This is another V-builder, the "V" being the slope of shoulders to waist. It is aimed at the shoulder muscles and upper back. It's also a good workout for the triceps, the muscles along the back of the upper arm.

Using two facing chairs, as in the shoulder dip, place the palms of your hands on the seats, and extend your legs in front of you, keeping them straight throughout the exercise. Now lower yourself between the chairs until your hips are only a few inches above the floor, then push up to arm's length.

You can make this reverse dip more effective by using a low footstool for your feet, but don't elevate them on a third chair; that would present a problem in balance which might result in severe muscle strain.

Again, begin with the number of repetitions that do not strain you, and increase gradually over a period of five weeks until you reach a goal of twenty-five repetitions.

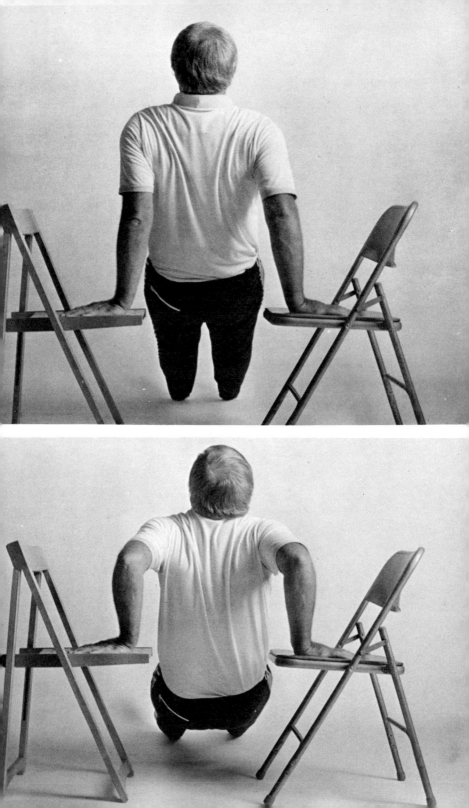

The Towel Press. If you've ever been on Muscle Beach in California, you may have noticed that the body-beautiful devotees are never without a towel in their hands. They are forever tugging it this way and that. It is not idle habit. They are building more muscle every minute.

The ordinary bath towel is an excellent piece of equipment in your "home gym." Used correctly, it will expand the muscles at the outer edge of your shoulders, build up the forearms and also build up the muscles on the underside of your shoulder blades. But the main job of this exercise is the creation of powerful triceps, the muscle which makes up two thirds of your upper arm.

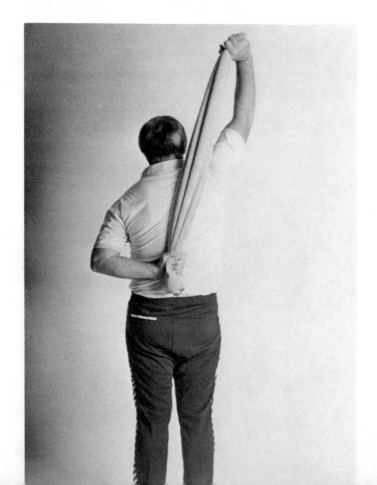

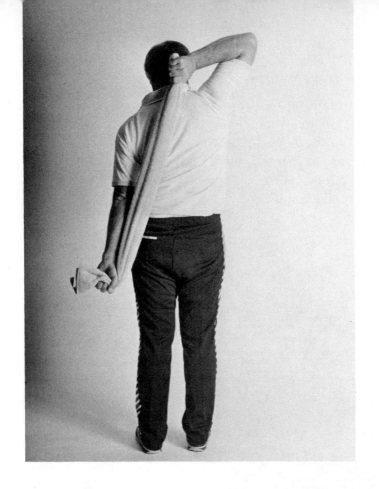

Grasp the opposite ends of a rolled towel in each hand and hold it behind your back so that your left forearm is across the small of your back and your right arm is extended straight overhead. The palm of your left hand is facing away from your body as you grasp the towel. Now, resisting with your right arm, pull the towel downward with your left hand until your right forearm is across the back of your head and your left arm is extended straight downward. Next, resisting with your left hand, pull upward with your right hand until you have returned to the starting position. Then switch the position of your hands, so that the right forearm is across the small of the back and your left arm is straight overhead. Repeat as before.

It's difficult to advise you on the number of repetitions, because so much depends on how much resisting pressure you put on yourself. A goal of ten hard-working repetitions, each side, is sufficient.

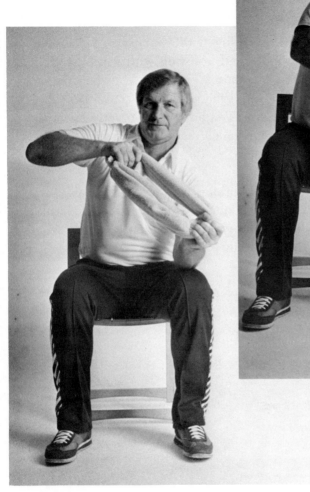

The Towel Curl. The mighty biceps is the object of this exercise.

In a sitting position, brace your right elbow on your right thigh near the knee. Hold both ends of a towel in your left hand and grasp the loop of the towel in your right hand, palm up. Lean forward and pull downward with your left hand while resisting with your right. Next pull upward with your right hand, resisting with your left.

This is the old "make a muscle" motion. After finishing a session with the right arm, switch positions and repeat the workout with the left arm. The number of repetitions here is not as important as how much resistant pressure you can muster.

After a few weeks of working to your peak goals, the amount of time you spend doing these exercises will shrink to such a few minutes that you will be able to work them into your daily routine easily.

CHAPTER IX

What Am I Doing the Rest of My Life?

There comes a day when the proudest of men must look in the mirror and say: My friend, you've had it. Time to move on. To change directions. To abandon the playthings of the long-ago boy.

After twenty-six seasons in professional football, I finally had that chat with myself. But, frankly, the results were inconclusive. Part of me kept saying: You played a heckuva lot longer than anyone expected. You thought you were through in 1959, and every year beyond that was a gift, a bonus. You prepared yourself for this moment, working in sales and marketing. So go quietly. Go placidly amid the noise and haste.*

But I heard another voice, the one that told me the calendar was a liar; I could still play, still kick. Who says it

*From the *Desiderata*, another line of which reads: "Take kindly the counsel of years, gracefully surrendering the things of youth."

113

can't go on forever? When you retire from the one job you ever cared about, the feeling is like getting run over by a Winnebago. You know that it can happen, does happen, but you never expect it to happen to you.

Does anyone out there remember 1927? Calvin Coolidge was the President. Lindbergh flew across the Atlantic. Babe Ruth hit sixty home runs. It was the year I was born.

Remember 1949? The musical comedy *Oklahoma!* was playing on Broadway. Joe Louis was the heavyweight champion. Scientists, having mastered the atomic bomb, were fooling around with the H-bomb. It was the year I joined the Chicago Bears.

And 1970. There was a war dragging on in Vietnam. The nation was divided over marijuana and the midiskirt. The economy was in trouble. And that year I came off the bench to kick the points and throw the touchdown passes that gave the Oakland Raiders three wins and a tie in the space of five weeks.

There was a story out of the Oakland training camp in 1976 that described how a rookie kicker from Boston College, Fred Steinfort, approached me in front of my locker. He introduced himself. I looked up and said, "I know who you are." Those were just about the last words we spoke to each other.

I had nothing against the rookie; at least, no more than any veteran has against any rookie. But I did resent the fact —understandably, I thought—that I had been told I had a job for that season, and in camp I was not allowed to compete for it. I had played twenty-six seasons and scored 2,002 points. Had spent ten of those years, mostly frustrating ones, trying to prove to George Halas in Chicago that I was a winner. Had gone to Houston, taken part in the birth of the American Football League and quarterbacked the team that won its first two championships. Released in Houston, I started over in Oakland, and one week before the 1970 season I found myself on the taxi squad. Yet that was the season of my so-called last-minute heroics. Death and resurrection indeed.

Many of my friends said what a shame it was that I didn't get to finish the season with Oakland in 1976, play on a winning Super Bowl team and then retire. But they missed the point. I would have wanted to play on one more. And then another. No matter when the time came I would not have been ready, not emotionally. They would have had to get rid of me exactly as they finally did: by sneaking my uniform out of the locker when I wasn't looking.

Doesn't everybody go through an adjustment of this kind, at some point? Age. Health. A change of life. Or the boss calls you in, coughs and says, "Sorry, Joe Lunchbox, but we're bringing in a new man from Kansas City to take over your department."

One hears a lot these days about a condition called the "midlife crisis." As I understand it, the crisis strikes between thirty-five and forty-five. In essence, it amounts to how we react to the discovery that our life is half gone, and the dreams that burned so strong at twenty may never be fulfilled. We may never be rich or famous, write a book, own the company, or become the youngest governor of Idaho.

How you respond depends in part on your physical and mental health. I don't think you can separate them. If you can get it together, the best years of your life will still be ahead of you.

Woody Allen said he faced his midlife crisis at forty, when he realized he would never be a pro athlete. "We are all taught to value the mind over the body," he said. "Just the opposite should be true. Achievements of the mind are full of complexities and self-delusions. When we see athletes do something perfect, it's very pure and genuine. You can't fool The Body."

It isn't always easy to tell when Allen, actor, comic writer, director, is putting us on. But he is a fanatic about sports and there is some truth in what he says.

Another park-bench philosopher, the old baseball pitcher Satchel Paige, once gave the world a lasting piece of wisdom when he said, "Don't look back, something may be gaining on you." But Satch was also into a fitness program, as reflected by these other "rules": "Avoid fried meats which angry up the blood." "If your stomach disputes you, lie down and pacify it with cool thoughts." "Keep the juices moving by jangling around gently as you walk." "Go light on the vices such as carrying on in society."

Satchel offered a sixth commandment, "Avoid running at all times," but we can overlook that one, which no doubt was inspired by medical opinion of another era, before jogging became acceptable.

I haven't had a midlife crisis in the classic sense. At least, I don't think so. I found my career as a football player ended at the age of forty-nine, and it dawned on me I was too *old* to go into coaching. I had treated the thought as a joke when I was playing, but now I realized it was true. I had majored in education at Kentucky. Had planned to teach or coach, or both. But if you don't start a coaching career by the time you are thirty, or at the latest thirty-five, you are just too far behind. There are so many people qualified to coach coming out of college every year.

When I left the training camp of the Raiders in 1976

and returned to my home in Chicago, I was faced with several decisions. If you find yourself at a similar crossroad, I recommend that you do what I did: put them off. If you can afford to wait, if you are not under financial pressures, avoid making a hurried decision that may rearrange your life.

My wife and I sat down and talked about our future. Money was not a problem. I had a busy speaking schedule. Television commercials for Chrysler and Grecian Formula 610. Offers in sales and public relations from several companies. Some cash in the bank. A few solid investments. And an NFL pension plan I could tap whenever I needed it. I was in a position, if I wanted, to start a company of my own.

The fact was, I didn't have the right answer yet. So my wife and I decided that we would take a year off to do whatever we wanted—to travel, play golf or pull weeds in the garden. As I write this, the year isn't up yet.

I am at a strange age, forty-nine, to be starting a second career. I honestly can't say what I will be doing fifteen years from now, or even five. But I do know one thing: I will continue to keep myself in top physical condition. Whatever you do, the transition will be easier if you have confidence in how you look and feel.

I have broken into four parts a program for anyone turning forty (or fifty) who is changing careers or facing retirement:

1. Just as you would have your car serviced for a holiday trip, tune up your body.

You used to hear a lot about athletes going to seed, not taking care of themselves after their active careers were finished. Some fellows would get so fat they had to have their shirts made by the Omaha Tent and Awning Company. In some ways, this was a response to all those years of regimentation. They would go to the other extreme. I don't see much of that anymore. Now, as I travel around the country, I run into old friends, former players, who weigh less now than when they played. Bob Asher, who weighed 260 at the peak of his career with the Bears, slimmed down to 230. Chuck Bednarik, Sam Huff, Bill George and George Connor, among many others, stay trim and active. Most athletes are intelligent enough to know you can't carry those extra pounds, over a period of years, once you no longer need them for padding. Your heart won't take it.

2. Find a routine. Regulate yourself. Free time is fine, but a sense of order can keep you from feeling your life is aimless.

When I retired from football, I found I had time to enjoy the things I wanted. My golf game is down to a six handicap. I can run my two miles in the morning without feeling that I should be somewhere else. I have time to play tennis and lift weights and ride a bike after dinner with my wife and daughter. If you have been liberated from a nine-to-five job, look on your new freedom as a challenge. Everything will seem better if you have the right conditioning and attitude. The air smells cleaner. Your food tastes better. And your wife looks like Elke Sommer.

It is important to settle on the activities you enjoy, and can do. Boredom is one enemy. Another is the frustration of trying a task too difficult for you. Strike a balance between intake and output. Remember: eat well, but avoid junk and work off the calories.

Athletes tend to tinker with their bodies the way Arnold Palmer might tinker with a golf club in his workshop. Don't subject yours to too many experiments. It takes a toll. Rosey Grier, the great defensive tackle for the Los Angeles Ram, was a great one for new diets. Trying to whittle himself down to three hundred pounds or so, Rosey was often in periods of feast or famine. One year he tried what he called "the teensy system," that is, subsisting on tiny portions. When he was overcome by the urge to have, say, ice cream with nuts, he would allow himself one spoon, topped by one nut.

The system might work for some, but not for Rosey. The next year he switched to another diet, and lost thirty pounds living on cottage cheese, peaches and broiled hamburger, meanwhile running three miles up a mountain four times a week. "When I felt the need for pastry," he said, "it was no longer necessary to taste a few crumbs. I ate a whole German chocolate cake. This satisfied my mind."

Ah, but what did it do to his body?

"It was okay," said Rosey, "as long as I kept running up the mountain."

3. Get your head on straight. Don't deceive yourself. Don't agonize over what-might-have-been and choices already made. If you find yourself in a transition from the one role you have performed best, the one you have prepared yourself to do all your life, I can empathize with you. A doctor doesn't have to give up medicine even if he can no longer perform brain surgery. A writer can write until the day he dies, if he can remember the alphabet and find a pencil. But a football player, among a few others, knows he has a limited time and he must come to terms

with that reality. The money is immaterial. It is the head-wrench of having to give up what you have done most of your life. Suddenly it is no longer there.

Athletes are proud people, most of whom find it hard, if not impossible, to admit they can't compete anymore. It is hard to give up the camaraderie, the glamour, the feeling of being a part of something good, particularly a winning team, but even a losing one. People spend their lives looking for clubs to join. A pro football team is one of the most exclusive of all. So you must be honest with yourself. All the money in the world won't take the place of a healthy mental attitude.

When you make a break with your past, this can be an ideal time to unload some excess luggage. Get rid of the regrets, grudges and angers that are the cargo of a long career. I made my own peace years ago with George Halas, the patriarch of the Chicago Bears, who consigned me to limbo in 1959. Now, I have never said this to Halas, but I think I understand him, and I admire what he and the other old-timers—Art Rooney and the late George Marshall —contributed to the game. There would be no pro football today without Halas. But I played three seasons without getting a raise, and when I asked for another five hundred dollars he reacted as though I was some kind of subversive. I thought then that he was merely cheap and ruthless. I know now that he was just trying to survive. He just didn't have a lot of money to toss around.

I will always be indebted to George for at least one of the lessons he pounded into us. He kept telling us to use our names and our time, make a business connection, save some money, invest. Pro football was only a start in life. It wasn't meant to insure your perpetual security.

Some of the people close to the Bears always said that we were too much alike to get along. I thought George was wrong for not playing me more. But I learned from him.

One day, in a game against the Chicago Cardinals, the crowd started yelling, "We want Blanda! We want Blanda!" Halas turned to me on the bench and said, "Hey, kid, you better get up in the stands. They want you."

4. Develop other interests. Establish new goals.

In all of my years on the field, I tried not to let my helmet get so crammed with *x*'s and *o*'s that I didn't know what was happening on page one. I made it a point to keep up with the stock market and politics. It's a cliché, I know, but everyone needs a hobby, an outlet. No matter what yours is —whether you garden, paint, rebuild cars or collect string —your mind needs that island of time. People who get so involved in an eighteen-hour-a-day job, and exclude everything else, are among those who fall quickly into the Type-A heart attack category. Nothing will put you away faster.

As a football player, I never set individual goals. Teams win championships, not players. Not until the year before it happened did I give any thought to ever holding the all-time scoring record, with 2,002 points. For one thing, I never expected to be a kicker. I didn't kick for the Bears until the latter part of my third season. I took on the job in Houston because there wasn't anyone else.

No doubt I missed a lot of the fun in football because I was so serious about it. I suppose I developed my ideas about the game from Coach Bear Bryant. Someone once asked him where he got his consuming drive to win, win, win. Coach Bryant tried to articulate what he thought, started over a half-dozen times, threw up his hands and finally said, "Hell, I don't know. All I know is, if someone has on a different colored jersey than me I want to whip his ass."

When I competed against someone he was my enemy. I never talked to opponents before a game, even if we had played on the same team in college.

Now, obviously, you spend some twenty-odd years developing that kind of mentality, and you need a decompression chamber when your career is over, in order to return to society. Sam Huff, the great New York Giants linebacker, once said that when you started carrying your anger with you all year long, that was when you knew it was time to retire.

"From the minute practice starts in July, until the season ends," said Huff, "you make yourself *mean*. You get mad. You say, 'To hell with them all. Look out for ole Sam Huff. He's mean today.' Then you go home and—boom!—you have to change your whole way of living in ten minutes. I remember after the first year, my wife and I went to a dance down home and there was this guy who kept rubbing his hand over the top of my brush-cut. Well, he did that twice and I got ready to give him a bang. But I had to remember where I was. For a few weeks or so, it was hard to calm down. It was harder the next year. It gets easier to be mean every year. Pretty soon there's no in-between. You're mean all year round. That's when you've been in pro football too long."

Well, yes, we do change, all of us. How much depends in part on how sharply your new circumstances differ from the old. One way or another, we all have to adjust: from giving orders or taking them; from being motivated by others or doing it on our own. The incentive isn't gone just because a job ends. There is a larger game. And the stake in it is to lead a better, fuller, longer life.

For me, football is gone but I have to keep myself in shape, lower my weight, and stay active because I want to enjoy the fruits of what I have accomplished. I saw my dad work hard all his life just to get to a point where he could relax. Of course, learning to relax is another trick. You have to begin by not feeling guilty.

When the pro golfer Julius Boros was asked if he planned to retire, he laughed out loud. "Retire from what?" he asked. "All I do now is fish and play golf."

So the good life is relative. But it does take discipline to follow a program, and self-discipline is never easy. You must make exercise and a sensible diet a *natural* part of your day, as much of a habit as brushing your teeth, so that if you skip a turn you feel uneasy.

Rest and sleep are essential. During the football season I was always in bed by eleven o'clock. To any executive who can, I recommend that you take a fifteen-minute nap in midafternoon, a fine way to relieve deskbound tension.

One of the oldest expressions in football is the definition of luck: When preparation meets opportunity. So perhaps I should pause here for a little story time. I can think of any number of incidents that illustrate the point, stories about athletes whose splendid fitness actually saved their lives.

There is a classic one about Ernie Stautner, an all-pro lineman for years with the Pittsburgh Steelers. Before one game Ernie had a muscle spasm, and the team doctor—a society doctor, a friend of the owner—gave him a muscle relaxant during the warm-ups. The doctor blundered. He had mixed ampules and given Stautner a lethal dose of a drug called Demerol. Ernie passed out, went into convulsions and had to be rushed to the hospital. When his coach, Buddy Parker, heard the news he was shocked. "Now, isn't that something to happen to a *coach*," he groaned, "losing one of your top players just before the kickoff?"

At the hospital, interns sent for a priest to administer the last rites. He leaned down and said, "I have come to hear your confession, my son."

Stautner opened an eye and whispered, "Okay, father, but I don't have much time, so if it's all the same to you I'll only hit the highlights."

Stautner pulled through, thanks, the doctors said, to his amazing constitution and physical conditioning. Ernie was part of what strikes me now as a more romantic time, when the players cared more about making the team than making the paycheck. In those years, mainly the 1950s, the players had limited freedom, but they made up for it by making less money.

We thought of some really creative ways to kill time. Some of the teams used to sponsor eating contests. On the Baltimore Colts one year, Gino Marchetti was matched against Don Joyce, a wrestler in the off season, with nearly five hundred dollars in bets on the table. Gino was outclassed by Joyce, who put away thirty-six pieces of chicken, plus peas and mashed potatoes by the gallon. Some witnesses say he even ate the bones. When the match was over Joyce poured a glass of ice tea, then reached into his pocket and dropped in two packets of saccharin. He looked up and explained, "I got to watch my weight."

Those days are gone forever, at least in pro football. I played the game for twenty-six years, and I wish, for those who keep asking, I had a more dramatic or colorful way of explaining how I lasted so long. But the truth is, you have only one body, and if you take care of it one is enough.

One final piece of advice. Don't let a clock or a calendar govern your life or your career. Age really is a state of mind. When I broke into pro football, the reigning heroes were Sammy Baugh, Bill Dudley, Bulldog Turner, George McAfee, Steve Van Buren. There were oldtimers hanging on, like Ted Fritsch and Indian Jack Jacobs, who were links to the era of Thorpe and Nagurski and Grange. In football, they were calling me an old man at thirty-one, and now, at forty-nine, I'll be a rookie at whatever business I decide to enter.

With the Bears, I played behind Johnny Lujack and Sid Luckman, when the team was still known as "the Monsters of the Midway." In Houston, I quarterbacked the first championship team the American Football League ever had. I went to the Super Bowl with Oakland after the '68 season, and in 1970, over a period of five weeks, I had the kind of surge that small boys have in their dreams.

I took a lot of memories out of pro football, and a philosophy: stay fit and think tough. When I joined the Bears in 1949, the payroll of the entire team was less than $350,000. Today they pay that much to some of the players. But I don't worry about having come along too soon, or too late. I don't look back. The important thing is to say I have been there. I did what I wanted most to do, and I consider myself a lucky man. I outlasted most of my critics.

I made the last field goal I ever attempted, a forty-two-yarder, with eight seconds to go in a losing playoff game against Pittsburgh, in 1975. And the last time I started at quarterback, in 1968, against Denver, I threw four touchdown passes, one to Warren Wells that went ninety-four yards, the longest in Oakland's history. I was forty-one years old. As I came off the field, with the score 40–7, I ran past the coach, John Rauch, and I pointed to the team's third quarterback, Cotton Davidson, age thirty-six. And I yelled over to Rauch, "Why don't you give the kid a little experience?"

CHAPTER X

Ask the Doctor

It is an American characteristic to ask questions. We want to know why things happen, how they work, what makes other people tick. In my lifetime in pro football I have answered my share, most of them having to do with why *that* pass wasn't completed, or what went through my mind as I lined up a kick.

As the years passed, people began to ask my opinion on subjects I had always taken for granted: fitness and survival. I had cheated the calendar. The Dorian Gray of football, they called me. I was still active in my forties in a sport where a fellow can get his neck wrung if he doesn't belong.

I've touched on all the main points of the exercise programs that can lengthen your life. But, undoubtedly, a lot of your questions remain unanswered. To cover this area, Dr. Reedy and Dr. Reginald Cherry, of Houston—where

I spent seven years with the Oilers—provided a list of the questions most often asked by people starting a fitness program. Dr. Cherry is a former associate of Dr. Ken Cooper.

Much of this book is based on the concept of exercise medicine, a relatively new field. The answers to these questions will help explain my objectives, and yours:

Q. How important is having a physical?

A. It's only by doing an annual physical that you can find the potential for developing disease. Screening methods are a way of looking at the future. There are two purposes of a physical examination: One, traditionally, is to determine the problems that exist right now—what's wrong with you, do you have a complaint, is there a disease present? Two is a new approach to a physical examination. It is to look to the future, to be able to predict what is going to happen ten years down the road. This is where so many physicals fall short. They stop with the first factor. One of the basic ingredients in looking at the future is developing some sort of table and tabulating your risks, predicting what will happen if your life style continues unchanged.

Q. Can exercise alone solve my health problems?

A. No. It must be coupled with diet. If you continue eating a lot of dairy products, exercise will not lower that cholesterol level. On the other hand, a lot of people go to different dietary programs in an attempt to lose weight without exercise. You can lose pounds right away, but without exercise you will gain them back as soon as you go off the diet. Looking at a number of factors and how they interact is important. There is no one thing that you can single out that kills people.

Q. When should a person start having a physical?

A. Generally, the acceleration phase of heart disease, which is the biggest killer, occurs in the early twenties. So it is recommended that by the late twenties people begin to concentrate on some sort of screening exam that looks at this potential risk. An exam every other year starting at age twenty-five is advisable. After thirty-five you need one every year. The reason is that doctors are seeing so many symptoms of heart disease in people in their lower thirties. They are seeing airline pilots with signifiant coronary-artery disease. One of the mechanisms that you use to detect this is the stress test. A resting electrocardiogram is helpful in only 15 percent of the people. It will miss that many with abnormal heart disease. The stress test *must* be done.

Q. At what age should a stress test be done?

A. If you are old enough to have a complete physical exam, you are old enough to have a stress test. It should be repeated every year, or at least every other year, in the case of a man over thirty-five and a woman over forty.

Q. How do you tell if your situation has reached a danger point?

A. Too often you can't. It is a paradox that it is a presumably "healthy person" who has a heart attack. That is, a person who has had no specific pain. For 55 percent of those with heart disease, the only warning is sudden death.

What this suggests is the redefinition of what is a healthy person. A victim probably had some risk-factor abnormalities. They were probably minor or he would have been treated for them, but stacked together they represent an overwhelming risk and they cannot be looked at singly. They must be graded as a group.

Q. Like what?

A. A cholesterol count of more than 220, finding a blood pressure of 145/95, a triglyceride level of 150, glucose of 120. Every one of these things in itself is not high enough for most physicians to treat with medicine. Your doctor wouldn't treat you for that cholesterol count, for that blood pressure, for that glucose. Yet stacked together this fellow is at a tremendous risk of heart disease and needs a different kind of therapy prescribed. And this is the realm of what we are talking about, a prescription for exercise and diet.

Q. If I'm a borderline patient, what is my risk?

A. These are the most perplexing patients. If a guy has a cholesterol level of 400, it gets the attention of the doctor and he is treated with medicine. If he has chest pain, he gets the attention of the doctor. But the statistics keep telling us: by and large heart attacks strike people with no symptoms.

Q. Besides the heart, what other problems should we be aware of?

A. The biggest emphasis in preventive medicine is placed on heart disease, secondarily on cancer prevention. A majority of cancers could be prevented if cigarette smoking were stopped. The other big factor in cancer is the incidence of colon cancer. The evidence is still not clear on the cause of colon cancer, but it is probably related to diet, too high in refined sugars and carbohydrates and too low in crude fiber. Few controlled studies have been done to show that yet, but they are coming. Doctors are very skeptical about anything in which they have no ream of data to support it.

Q. I'm an executive. What type of unique prevention problems do I face as a result of stress?

A. The executive is faced with the same problems as everybody else—lack of exercise, diet, the stress factor. But the point must be made that it isn't stress itself that kills people. Our whole society is based on production, and stress can be a stimulus not only to the body but also to the intellect. The problem is the way we handle stress. We are simply not allowing an outlet for it. Exercise is being used by a lot of psychiatrists to treat anxious-depressive patients —an end stage of high-stress situations. So we need an outlet.

Q. What type of exercise?

A. Jogging is the most popular, if you consider both the time commitment and the heart benefits. But jogging is not for everyone. It is boring to a lot of people. Some have knee and ankle problems and can't jog. What we are talking about really is endurance exercises, anything that keeps the heart rate elevated and does not allow it to fall during the course of exercise—cycling, swimming, walking, jogging. Any aerobic exercise that can be done continuously for a period of time.

Q. So keeping the heart rate up seems to be the key?

A. Right. Even with walking, you can't stop at stop signs or intersections; you have to do it continuously, which is why so many exercises just don't qualify.

Q. If a program is followed, does it cut down on the amount of medications that one should be taking?

A. A lot of people could get off their medications if they followed an exercise program.

Q. What about the effects of alcohol?

A. There has been a lot of debate on alcohol. Some groups contend it increases the incidence of heart attacks. For a fact, it can cause cirrhosis, the fourth leading cause of death in men over the age of forty. But the biggest problem with alcohol is simply the caloric intake. It can be converted to triglycerides, which is another type of blood fat, and therein lies the worst risk. That, and the liver disease associated with alcohol.

Q. What about these low-carbohydrate diets, which award so few points for alcohol that it doesn't hurt you?

A. The drinking man's diet came out and was very popular. But, right or wrong, you must ask yourself, is the consumption of alcohol worth the potential harm? The hard stuff has no place in a good preventive-medicine program.

Q. What about the fact that you can get undersugared?

A. Not true. The body does convert protein and fat to sugar. You won't get undersugared.

Q. What about cigarettes? You say we could eliminate a majority of cancer if people stopped smoking. What else does it do to you?

A. It is one of the three big risk factors in heart disease, ranking right alongside cholesterol and blood pressure. The effects of smoking on small vessels are well known. It constricts them, and accelerates the deposition of cholesterol in the arteries. It is a very big risk factor.

Q. How do insurance companies treat preventive medicine?

A. One large insurance company has offered a 50 percent reduction in premiums on life insurance if the insured can meet certain risk criteria. If you qualify for the reduction, you must pay the full premium again any time one risk factor—say cholesterol—exceeds certain limits. Preventive medicine is cheaper in the long run. It saves a great deal of money, keeping people out of the hospital.

Q. Can exercise therapy change the actuary tables?

A. That depends on how well people are motivated. They have to be "scared" a little to get them started. Hopefully, studies in the future will show that exercise can affect the death rate from heart disease. The real tragedy is that heart disease is increasing markedly among men in their most productive years, in their forties and fifties.

Q. Is it a bad idea to exercise just before you go to bed?

A. Only to the extent that you need to allow time for a cool-down period after any kind of prolonged exercise. This means you may need to set aside up to thirty minutes before getting under the covers.

Q. I am untrained as a runner. Is my form important?

A. You are not qualifying for the Olympics, but, yes, form is always important. You should run heels first, with relaxed arm and elbow motion. Breathe as naturally as possible with your mouth open. Most beginning runners or joggers tend to be duckfooted, running with their feet apart. This can result in shin problems. The idea is to point your toes straight ahead. Run on as flat a surface as you can, keeping your stride perfectly level and relaxed.

Q. Does sex have any value as an aerobic activity?

A. Sex has the potential for being an aerobic exercise *if* one could maintain an elevated heart rate for a sustained period of time. Normally, what happens is a rapid increase in pulse rate and then a drop, not unlike tennis. Sex does not take the place of exercise. But the evidence tells us that exercise improves sex. If you attain your ideal weight, and feel better, you are going to perform more effectively in many different areas. An improved sex life is just one desirable side effect of being in shape.

Q. If I work with weights, and then stop, am I more prone to having a heart attack?

A. Pumping iron and developing big muscles condition the heart not one bit. But it is a myth that the body-beautiful types are more prime heart attack candidates if they stop. This notion goes along with the so-called "athlete's heart." A study of marathon runners, including Olympians Kenny Moore and Frank Shorter, showed they all had enlarged hearts—but super*normal* hearts. Some of them had resting pulse rates of 35 and 40 beats a minute. Their hearts were doing less work, because they pumped out such a large volume with each beat.

CHAPTER XI

Food That's Good for You and Food That's Good

Some Words About Good Nutrition

Proteins. The food element from which all body tissue is built, and therefore the most important ingredient in your diet. An abundance of protein is necessary for growth. The most efficient suppliers of protein: egg yolk, cheese, milk, yogurt, liver, kidney, sweetbreads, roasts, chops, steaks, soya beans, nuts, wheat germ and cottonseed flour. Less efficient but still plentiful suppliers of protein: dry beans, lentils, dry peas, corn, rye, gelatin and egg white.

Inadequate protein in your diet will lead to pale color of blood, low blood pressure, fatigue, poor muscle tone, faulty posture and low resistance to infection and disease.

Carbohydrates. The sweet and starchy foods that are most easily converted into fat by your body function— bread, cereals, potatoes, spaghetti. The danger—as far as weight gain can be termed a danger—is in adding unsaturated fats to the carbohydrates. That is, butter with potatoes. This will more than double the calorie total: one third of a pound of baked potato is 125 calories, and three quarters of an ounce of butter totals 188 calories, for a grand total of 313.

Cholesterol. A body chemical produced by the liver for many varied uses. The one that concerns us is its role in transporting fats in the bloodstream, leaving deposits just beneath the walls of the arteries, thereby narrowing the channel through which the blood flows. Cholesterol also tends to corrupt adjacent healthy cells, which develop scar tissue and further close up the artery. The medical evidence suggests that a high level of cholesterol clogs the artery and thereby invites high blood pressure. It is like placing your finger partway over the opening of a garden hose— you increase the pressure but cut down the flow.

Saturated Fat. This is a chemist's phrase to describe the connection of atoms. Saturated fat is a string of carbon atoms, each with two hydrogen atoms attached. It is the single most deadly cause of increased cholesterol. Unfortunately, the mainstays of America's famed "square meal" are loaded with saturated fats—beef, pork, butter, eggs (in fact, all dairy products except skim milk, buttermilk and cottage cheese); ordinary margarine, solid fats such as lard and hydrogenated shortening, plus the whole roster of flour products.

Unsaturated fat. If saturated fat is the bane, its cousin, unsaturated fat, is the boon. In unsaturated fat one of the atoms in the carbon string is minus one of its hydrogen hitch-hikers, a circumstance that actually lowers the cholesterol level. These fats are called polyunsaturated. Sources of polyunsaturated fats are few—fish and other nonshell seafood, pecans, peanuts, walnuts, whole grains, liquid vegetable cooking oils, special margarines and the natural oils from safflower, corn, cottonseed, sunflower and sesame.

Vitamins. A classification of substances that are not foods in themselves but that are necessary to nutrition and to the regulation of metabolic processes. Herewith a brief description of each vitamin:

Vitamin A. Always found in association with fat in the animal body. It is stored in the body and does not require daily replenishing. Milk, egg yolk, liver, cod-liver oil, lettuce, carrots, spinach, turnip tops are rich in vitamin A. White bread lacks it. This is the vitamin that provides a "glowing" complexion.

Vitamin B. Now known to be at least six different vitamins, including B_2, which has become known as vitamin G. The lack of vitamin B_1, or thiamine, causes irritableness and nervous disorders and, in extreme cases, beriberi. It is found abundantly in corn or wheat germ, yeast and rice polishings, as well as such common foods as milk, fresh fruits, whole-grain cereals, fresh vegetables and modern enriched flour and cereals. It must be replenished daily.

Vitamin C. Chemically, ascorbic acid, a vital ingredient to your all-around health, which will be satisfied by regular consumption of citrus fruit in all forms, juice and/or fresh, and by tomatoes, particularly the plum-size. Absence of vitamin C brings about scurvy. The body is unable to store vitamin C for any length of time, so keep it coming.

Vitamin D. In childhood, this ingredient prevents rickets. The most natural source is sunshine striking your bare skin. Fish and other seafoods are abundant edible sources. Vitamin D has been added to milk, and particularly to skim milk.

Vitamin E. All the functions of this vitamin are not known. But scientists believe it may be important to reproduction and beneficial to the heart if, as some believe, it tends to thin the blood. The best sources of vitamin E are wheat-germ oil, lettuce, whole-grain cereals, milk, eggs, liver and most vegetables.

Vitamin G. This is the antipellagric vitamin and, unlike B_1, is not destroyed by heat. It is abundant in milk, liver, yeast, lean beef, green leafy vegetables and bananas. Lack of vitamin G brings about stunted growth, loss of weight, and soreness of eyes, mouth and nose.

The other vitamins, such as P and K, are almost automatically included in your everyday intake of food, unless you are in a prisoner-of-war camp.

Some Recipes I've Liked

The complaint most often heard from people on a diet is the sameness and blandness of the menus they must suffer. Whether the goal is to lose weight or to avoid foods harmful to your health or shape, the dishes are too often unexciting.

Such a complaint is no longer valid. There are recipes now available fit for a gourmet, containing little or no cholesterol or carbohydrates. I have collected a few favorites of my own over the years, and I submit them now to prove that a diet regimen doesn't have to be unendurable.

These foods are so nutritious you will feel better just reading about them. Some years ago, in a cookbook sponsored by wives of players in the old American Football League, Fred Williamson of Kansas City gave away his recipe for forty quarts of minestrone. You start with two pounds of barley, three pounds of split peas, three pounds of dried lima beans, two bunches of celery, and three pounds of salt pork. Williamson's minestrone was the soup *du jour*—for the whole league. Needless to say, it is not recommended for those with special eating problems.

But there was one recipe, provided by a player's wife, worth passing on to the lady in your kitchen: "A good many husbands are spoiled by mismanagement. Some women keep them constantly in hot water; others let them freeze by their carelessness and indifference. Some keep them in a stew with irritating ways and words. Some wives keep them pickled, while others waste them shamefully. But they are really delicious when prepared properly."

Read, and eat, on:

Step up to the health bar and have a few on the house. No matter how strict your diet, there are dozens of excellent dishes that can be prepared to vary your menu without violating your restrictions. The recipes selected here have two advantages: they are all tasty, and most of them can be handled by the guy who doesn't know a cheese grater from an egg beater.

Tuna Fish Mexican Style

1 tomato, chopped	½ avocado
1 tablespoon chopped onion	1 can tuna fish
½ jalapeno pepper, chopped	3 onion rings
	2 small romaine leaves
1 teaspoon chopped parsley	3 radishes

Mix the chopped tomato, onion, jalapeno and parsley together and place on dinner plate. Chop the avocado over the mixture, top with tuna hunks and garnish with onion rings, romaine leaves and radishes.

Salmon-Stuffed Avocado

1 avocado	1 tablespoon chopped parsley
2 tablespoons lemon juice	2 tablespoons chopped tomato
1 cup (8 ounces) canned pink salmon	1 tablespoon mayonnaise
1 tablespoon finely chopped onion	2 slices jalapeno pepper salt and pepper
	¼ head lettuce

Cut the avocado in half lengthwise, remove the seed, and peel. Sprinkle with lemon juice. Combine the salmon, onion, parsley and tomato and toss with mayonnaise, salt and pepper. Pack mixture in seed cavity of avocado halves and garnish with one slice of jalapeno each. Serve on lettuce leaves.

High-Protein Chicken Dinner

chicken breast (1 per person)	½ cup chopped celery
2 carrots	¾ tablespoon chicken base
½ cup chopped onion	lettuce leaves
	1 tomato, sliced

Put chicken breast in boiling water to cover, add salt and pepper and simmer for 15 minutes. Add carrots cut in large pieces, onion, celery and chicken base and simmer for 20 minutes longer, until vegetables are done. Remove chicken and serve on plate with lettuce and tomato. Serve vegetable and liquid as soup.

Beef on a Shingle
(famous in World War II)

1 tablespoon corn oil	½ of an 8-ounce package dried beef
1½ tablespoons flour	2 slices gluten bread, toasted
½ cup skim milk	

This is a quick one. Pour oil in skillet over medium-range heat, add skim milk first and then the rest and keep stirring until the whole mess is pretty thick. Pour over toast.

The Fat Man's Cake

(Soya Muffins)

1½ cups soya flour	3 tablespoons brown sugar
2 teaspoons baking powder	1 tablespoon grated orange rind
1½ teaspoons vegetable salt	1½ cups milk
2 fresh eggs (or egg substitute)	1 tablespoon corn oil
	¼ cup floured raisins
	¼ cup floured walnuts

Sift flour, baking powder and salt. Separate eggs; beat yolks until very light and frothy. Add sugar, orange rind, milk and oil to yolks and mix well. Pour egg mixture into dry ingredients and mix. Add raisins and nutmeats and mix thoroughly. Fold in egg whites beaten stiff. Pour into small muffin tins and bake in slow oven (300° F.) for 35 minutes.

The astronauts eat their suppers in flight out of a toothpaste tube, and there has been a suggestion that the next space capsule be made out of edible parts. George Orwell and 1984, here we come.

It is only logical that the march of science, keeping one stride ahead of the race for the fast buck, should produce new discoveries in weight control. Somewhere in this profusion of excesses and extremes, help is available for the average guy who wants to help his body, get back to his normal weight *and stay there.* In this respect, athletic coaches and trainers are helpful to us because they are pragmatic: does it work or doesn't it? From their ranks has come an unqualified "yes" on great natural boosters such as wheat germ and a protein food supplement.

This plunges us into the subject of "food faddism," a phrase dieticians utter with a shudder. Their target is the nut who stuffs himself to the gills with every new gimmick that hits the health-food shelf, the fellow who ignores the fundamentals of good eating and thinks he has found a magic potion.

But there is a case for wheat germ and protein powder, and pleasant ways to consume them, as these recipes will demonstrate:

Wheat-Germ Muffins

1 cup whole-wheat flour	1 egg (or egg substitute)
2½ teaspoons baking powder	¼ cup soy oil
1 cup wheat germ	¼ cup honey
⅔ cup skim milk	½ cup raisins
	¼ cup chopped pecans (optional)

Sift whole-wheat flour and baking powder with pinch of salt and mix with wheat germ. Mix milk, egg, soy oil, and honey separately and then add to original dry ingredients and mix. Add raisins and nuts. Bake in muffin tin for 25 minutes with oven at 400° F. Serve with scoop of sherbet.

Blanda Special

10 strawberries (or 1 sliced fresh peach, pear or pineapple as you wish)	2 raw eggs (or egg substitute)
	2 heaping tablespoons honey

1 tablespoon high-
   protein powder
6 ounces skim milk

1 teaspoon wheat germ
½ cup crushed ice

Mix all the ingredients in a blender for two minutes. Serve in a 16-ounce glass. (A cocktail shaker may be used— a pretty good workout in itself.)

Vitamin-C Cooler

(A good sub for breakfast)

6 ounces grapefruit or
   orange juice
1 tablespoon honey
1 teaspoon wheat germ

1 tablespoon protein
   powder
5 drops lemon juice
½ cup crushed ice

Mix ingredients in blender for two minutes. Serve in a 12-ounce glass.

Tutti-Frutti Shake

4 ounces orange juice
2 tablespoons honey
¾ cup crushed ice

1 cup assorted chopped
   fruit (banana, straw-
   berry, apple, canta-
   loupe, watermelon,
   orange, pear, peach)

Mix in a blender for two minutes. Serve in a 10-ounce glass.

Vitamin-A Special

6 ounces orange juice	1 tablespoon protein
1 tablespoon honey	powder
juice of ½ lemon	½ cup crushed ice

Mix in blender for two minutes. Serve in a 10-ounce glass.

Yeast on the Rocks
(an antidote for hangovers)

3 tablespoons brewer's	6 ounces skim milk
yeast	½ slightly overripe banana
1 tablespoon honey	

Mix in blender for two minutes. Serve in a 10-ounce glass.

Most over-forties have a built-in prejudice against salads. They regard the fresh greenery with disdain and call it "rabbit food." But those who have to fight the battle of the bulge are missing a good bet. The trick is to begin with a huge salad as the first course of your main meal. In addition to being an aid to digestion, the low-calorie salad leaves less room in the appetite for the fattening courses that follow. Here are just two suggestions (the creative salad-maker can invent endless variations):

Tuna-Stuffed Tomatoes

2 tomatoes	1 tablespoon mayonnaise
1 can tuna fish	½ jalapeno pepper,
2 tablespoons chopped	chopped
onion	leaves of ¼ head of
1 teaspoon chopped	lettuce
parsley	2 or 3 slices cantaloupe or
	honeydew melon

Cut tomatoes partway in four sections and scoop out the insides. Mix tuna fish, onion, parsley, mayonnaise, jalapeno and place on lettuce bed. Garnish with melon slices.

Raw-Vegetable Salad

1 cup finely chopped	1 hard-boiled egg
spinach	1 tablespoon raisins
1 cup grated carrots	2 ounces olive oil
1 cup grated beets	juice of 1 lemon
1 tomato, sliced	

Place spinach, carrots and beets on separate parts of dinner plate, with tomato slices spaced between. Cut egg into four wedges and place in center. Put the raisins in the carrot portion. Sprinkle olive oil and lemon juice over the entire plate.

Polyunsaturated Mayonnaise
(How to make your own)

2 egg yolks	¾ cup corn oil
¼ teaspoon salt	1 tablespoon lemon juice
¼ cup olive oil	

Mix egg yolks and salt in automatic mixer and add the oils slowly from a tablespoon until mixture starts to thicken. Add lemon juice after adding the oil. Note: pink mayonnaise can be made with 1 tablespoon of powdered pimento, and "hot" mayonnaise with a New Orleans flavor can be made by adding 1 teaspoon of dry mustard and dashes of Louisiana hot sauce.

For those on a strict low-cholesterol diet, these recipes are offered to break the monotony of your limited fare:

All-Purpose Dip
(appetizer)

½ bouillon cube	2 cups low-fat cottage
¼ cup hot water	cheese
	½ teaspoon onion salt

Dissolve bouillon cube in hot water. Place all ingredients in a blender. Blend until smooth. May be used as a spread, a dip or a canapé. Yield: 2¼ cups.

Variations: Add any of the following: 2 tablespoons chopped chives; ⅛ teaspoon garlic powder; 2 tablespoons chopped olives; 1 tablespoon chili sauce, plus drop of Tabasco.

Italian Spinach Soup

1 package (10½ ounces) frozen spinach	1 tablespoon salt
¼ cup water	¼ teaspoon white pepper
2 tablespoons oil	⅛ teaspoon nutmeg
¼ cup minced onion	6 cups water
1 clove garlic, minced	3 tablespoons corn meal

Steam spinach in ¼ cup water as indicated on package. Drain. Purée cooked spinach in blender. Heat oil in saucepan and sauté onion and garlic in it. Blend in salt, pepper and nutmeg. Add puréed spinach and 6 cups of water; bring ingredients to a rolling boil and stir in corn meal. Simmer 30–35 minutes, stirring frequently.

Yield: 6 servings.

Spanish Cabbage

2 tablespoons margarine	1 small cabbage, thinly sliced
1 small onion, thinly sliced	1 small bell pepper, thinly sliced
⅔ cup tomatoes, chopped	2 teaspoons salt

Melt margarine in a large saucepan and sauté the onion in it. Add remaining ingredients plus ¼ cup water. Cover and cook on high heat until steam begins to escape from around edges of lid. Reduce heat to low and cook for 20 minutes, or until tender.

Yield: 6 servings.

Polynesian Pineapple Chicken

2 whole chicken breasts, boned and skinned	3 tablespoons oil
¾ teaspoon salt	1 tablespoon cornstarch
¼ teaspoon white pepper	2 tablespoons soy sauce
2 tablespoons cornstarch	2 teaspoons lemon juice
1 can (16 ounces) pineapple chunks	

Cut chicken breasts into 2-inch pieces. Mix salt, pepper and 2 tablespoons cornstarch; toss chicken pieces in this mixture. Drain pineapple, reserving ¾ cup juice. Heat oil in skillet; sauté chicken 10–15 minutes, until it is golden brown. Add pineapple chunks; cover and simmer 5–6 minutes. Mix 1 tablespoon cornstarch, soy sauce, lemon juice and pineapple juice. Add to chicken, stirring until the sauce begins to boil. Cook 2–3 minutes, being careful not to overcook.

Yield: 4 servings.

Strawberry Cheesecake

graham cracker crust	1 teaspoon grated lemon rind
egg substitute equivalent to 1 egg	2 tablespoons lemon juice
¼ cup sugar	1 teaspoon vanilla
1 tablespoon cornstarch	3 cups low-fat cottage cheese
¼ teaspoon salt	

1 cup skim milk
2 tablespoons unflavored gelatin
¼ cup cold water
2 egg whites
⅓ cup evaporated skim milk, chilled
⅓ cup sugar
10 fresh strawberries

Whip egg substitute for 5 minutes and set aside. In saucepan, combine ¼ cup sugar, cornstarch, and salt. Gradually add skim milk and heat to boiling, stirring constantly. Remove from heat and allow to set for 3 minutes. Add egg substitute, stirring constantly. Soften gelatin in cold water and add to milk mixture. Add lemon rind, lemon juice, and vanilla. Let stand at room temperature until mixture begins to set. Force cottage cheese through a sieve or process with electric mixer or in blender until smooth. Fold cottage cheese into thickened gelatin mixture. Beat egg whites until soft peaks form; gradually add ⅓ cup sugar. Whip chilled evaporated skim milk until soft peaks form. Fold egg whites and whipped milk into gelatin mixture and spoon into graham cracker crust. Refrigerate until firm. Arrange fresh strawberries on top of cheesecake.

Yield: 10 servings.

All-American Pink-Lemonade Pie

1 9-inch baked pie shell
1 cup evaporated skim milk
1 envelope (¼ ounce) unflavored gelatin
¼ cup cold water
1 can (6 ounces) frozen pink-lemonade concentrate, thawed
¾ cup sugar

Chill evaporated milk in freezer until ice crystals begin to form around edges. Chill bowl and electric-mixer beaters. Soften gelatin in cold water in 1-quart saucepan. Add lemonade and simmer until gelatin dissolves. Add sugar, stirring until dissolved, but not thickened. Cool. Beat chilled evaporated milk in chilled bowl at high speed until it is stiff. Fold into the cooled gelatin mixture. Pour into pie shell and chill 3–4 hours or until firm.

Yield: 8 servings.

Crumb Crust

1 cup graham cracker crumbs	¼ cup sugar
2 tablespoons margarine, melted	⅛ teaspoon nutmeg
	¼ cup chopped pecans (optional)

Combine ingredients and mix well. Press into a 9-inch round cake pan. Place in 350° F. oven for 1 minute. Chill in refrigerator until crust is well firmed. Use for cream pies, cheesecake, etc.

Yield: 12 servings in 9-inch round cake pan.

Margarine Pastry

1 cup flour	½ cup margarine
½ teaspoon salt	2–3 tablespoons cold water

Mix flour and salt. Cut in margarine until coarse-meal texture is obtained. Sprinkle with water, mixing gradually.

Form into ball. Chill about 10 minutes. Roll out. Preheat oven for 10 minutes at 425° F., and then bake for 12–15 minutes.

Postscript

I had thought of winding up the book by letting you see the off-season conditioning program recommended by the Oakland Raiders. My thought was that it would give you an idea of the activity professional football players go through when they are *taking it easy*.

But I had second thoughts, even though you might have found in it some exercises that could be adapted to your needs. On the whole, they are too strenuous, too exhausting, and simply too much for anyone to try to maintain every day, year in and year out. Your body needs rest periods at any age, and you can absolutely burn yourself out. Even professional athletes can.

What is more, athletes have one problem very similar to what we over-forty civilians have. They may be advised to work just as hard in the off season and they may claim they do, but it simply is not true. You never work as hard alone as you do when you are in a group and the adrenalin is going. So, again, I urge you to join a jogging club, or an exercise class at the Y, or recruit three or four friends to work out with you along the sensible lines indicated in this book.

If you find the right company, and maintain the right pace for even a few minutes a day, you won't need any better off-season program.